Theodore Augustus Barry, Benjamin Adam Patten

Men and Memories of San Francisco

Theodore Augustus Barry, Benjamin Adam Patten

Men and Memories of San Francisco

ISBN/EAN: 9783744669658

Printed in Europe, USA, Canada, Australia, Japan

Cover: Foto ©ninafisch / pixelio.de

More available books at **www.hansebooks.com**

MEN AND MEMORIES

OF

SAN FRANCISCO,

IN THE

"SPRING OF '50."

BY

T. A. BARRY AND B. A. PATTEN.

"Forsan et hæc olim meminisse juvabit."—VIRGIL.

SAN FRANCISCO:
A. L. BANCROFT & COMPANY,
PUBLISHERS, BOOKSELLERS AND STATIONERS.
1873.

Entered according to Act of Congress, in the year 1873, by
A. L. BANCROFT & COMPANY,
In the Office of the Librarian of Congress, at Washington.

PREFACE.

Years ago it was no unfrequent thing for old *residentes*, who, in the course of conversation, had arrived at a point of doubt or difference upon the location of some building, or the names of its occupants, their personal appearance, profession, or peculiarities in the "Spring of '50," to come to us for information on the mooted point, believing that our long continued residence and peculiar opportunities for observation, together with unusually good memories, rendered our decisions worthy of consideration. As Time's incessant revolution whirls us on and on, still farther from those days, and looking back upon the long vista of years, the once familiar spots and well-known forms and faces fade in the distance. These inquiries increase day by day, and so often have we been correct, that many of our friends have said: "Write some of the reminiscences of those old times, and we will read them." Disclaiming all merit in these pages, save their mnemonic faithfulness, we offer them to the kind consideration of our friends and the public.

B. & P.

SAN FRANCISCO, May, 1873.

MEN AND MEMORIES

OF

SAN FRANCISCO IN THE SPRING OF '50.

MEN AND MEMORIES

OF

SAN FRANCISCO IN THE SPRING OF '50.

CHAPTER I.

The man who has lived in San Francisco for nearly a quarter of a century; who has never been absent from it longer than two weeks in all these years; who can recall vividly all the old and once familiar streets and buildings, and the men who lived in them, can always command attention from those whose memory, less active and retentive, is ever latent and easily awakened with an eager and peculiar pleasure to listen to the reminiscences of the early days.

Disappointment may await the reader who expects any literary merit in these pages; but we think that he who searches them for facts long laid away and forgotten in the dusty folios of memory's by-gone years, will find but few paragraphs that will prove uninteresting.

There is a romance attached to the early days of San Francisco's history, a real interest clinging to the men who lived here, and to the incidents of their lives during those strange, eventful days—something not so easily explained to those who were not here—a kind of freemasonry, binding fraternally all those who lived here in a time when the very sense of remoteness and isolation from all the rest of the world brought men closer together; made men who knew each other merely by name, and who had never spoken together, grasp each other's hands and form life-long friendships, born of a sympathy in men so similarly circumstanced, drawn to one field by eager, adventurous enterprise, such a long, weary way from home and loved ones, having something in common, so different from any previous experience known or read of by men.

Although nearly a quarter of a century has elapsed, the kindly sentiment still burns in the hearts of these men. Even the scapegrace and vagabond of to-day, who happened to be here in the early days, retains, somehow, a place in the hearts of his more fortunate and respectable pioneer brethren, who never forget that he is a '49-er, or, better still, more remotely dates his advent. A resident of those days will linger and courteously endure the bore of the most dilapidated specimen of humanity, with a forbearance bordering on the marvelous in the eyes of those who were not here, and to whom the whole thing is more mysterious than freemasonry. If a man who came to San Francisco subsequent to 1850 should venture a hint that time and money given to such objects were worse than wasted, he will be met with a "Yes, yes, exactly! but you don't quite understand it, and it isn't to be expected that you should! you were not here in those days, you know! You see, there's a kind of feeling toward the men of that time, however unfortunate since, which—eh, well!— we can't see those men in want, and what little we give them is of no consequence." And with a wave of the hand, and a half apologetic, half deprecatory shrug of the shoulders, our friend too gladly dodges the truth. Still, he never will—not if he lives for a century to come—turn the cold shoulder upon one of the "*Old-time boys*," should Time permit the venerable loafer's lingering so long. While we may smile contemptuously—we of later days—still, we must admire this spirit, more than friendship, created under such peculiar circumstances and enduring through so many years.

There is a genuine regret, a kind of Pioneer-pity, in the hearts of some of the unmitigated '49-ers, for those unfortunate men whom cruel fate denied the ineffable glory of arriving in San Francisco in the memorable year of 1849; or who were not within three marine leagues of California's auriferous shores previous to the midnight of December, 31, 1849. Time cannot soften the hearts of these *otherwise* good old men towards those unhappy individuals who arrived here subsequent to that momentous period in the world's history. Messrs. Winant, Bond, Clark, Stout, M. D., and a very few others, are obdurate, and our only hope is in the liberal faction, headed by Messrs. Holland, Von Schmidt, Donahue, *et al.* The man who is hardened enough to confess that he did not see the traditional mule, foundered in the slough on Montgomery street, between Clay and Washington—the man who admits that he never saw the tide half way across Montgomery at the corner of Jackson—who has not walked on sidewalks made of sacks of flour and boxes of Virginia's finest tobacco—that man, we say, has no reason to expect the slightest consideration (*in a Pioneer way*) from those inexorable men of the '49 faction. We never could see the sense of the Pioneer Association, in celebrating the anniversary of California's admission into the Union. Why should such a body of men sanction the admission of California into the Union, when she didn't arrive there before midnight of the thirty-first of December, 1849? It is simply ridiculous, absurd, for them to notice the ninth of September, 1850; almost as inconsistent as electing to the presidency of the association a man who had the hardihood to delay his arrival in San Francisco until after the midnight of December 31, 1849.

The atmosphere becomes very foggy at times in the social room of the Pioneer's Association; and it was so most likely when Capt. Johns was elected to preside over men who left the east more suddenly, and arrived in the west on *better time* than he did. Some grave, deliberate bodies are comical without intention.

All just and fair-thinking men agree that everybody who was in California on the ninth of September, 1850, should be eligible for membership in the association of California Pioneers. Every man, woman or child who were here before the Territory became a State of the Union, is a pioneer. It is amusing to notice the sticklers for *cesta* among the '49ers, just among those who came in that year; among the earlier comers, the feeling does not exist.

The De Witts or Harrisons of '48 are not in the least jealous of those who came between January 1st, 1850, and September 9th, 1850. Col. Stevenson, James L. Wadsworth, Dr. Parker, Mr. Nuttman, are not; J. C. Denniston (peace to his memory) never was, being the personification of generosity; Messrs. Russ, father and sons, Alcalde Hyde, Alcalde Leavenworth, Judge Botts, nor any of those men of '46 and '47. The same may be said of the late Robert Parker, the late Judge Blackburn, and the late Harry Spiel, of Santa Cruz; of Major Snyder, Charley Southard, the late Major Hensley, John Sullivan, the Murphys and Mr. Thomas Fallon, and all the men of '44; or of Josiah Belden, Don José Thompson, Henry F. Teschemacher, and those of '41–'2–'3; of the late Thomas O. Larkin, the late Wm. D. M. Howard, and those of '39–'8–'7; and farther back to Jacob P. Leese, Don Juan Foster, Mr. Stokes, of Monterey, Mr. Branch, of San Luis Obispo; and still farther back, to Charley Brown, of Mission Dolores, who came here in '29; Captains Wilson and Dana, David Spencer and Captain Cooper, who came somewhere between the years '23 and '29; and we do not believe that Mr. Gilroy, who settled in California in 1814, would have voted against any pioneer of 1850.

In the following editorial, clipped from the San Francisco *Evening Bulletin*, Feb. 6, 1873, we find our own and the general public sentiment well and truly expressed. It was written by one who has earned the right to give his opinion upon the subject—one who arrived in San Francisco on the eighth of July, 1849, and worked for two or three months after his arrival as a boatman in the harbor, and subsequently served a full apprenticeship in the mines of our State; one who can handle rocker or cradle; is a good oarsman; a linguist; and a genuine connoisseur in art. As to his ability in journalistic matters, the subjoined editorial may be offered in evidence:

"WHAT MAKES A PIONEER"?

"Malvolio, musing in the garden, is incited to attempt his lady's favor by these oracular words: 'Some are born great, some achieve greatness, and some have greatness thrust upon them.' The world has worshipers enough for all these sorts of greatness, but as the larger number of people who desire its notice are not so lucky as to belong to either the first or last of the specified classes, they are compelled to earn distinction by some act of their own. Various are the roads to fame. Some men write poems, while others stand on their heads for it. Some 'wade through slaughter to a throne,' while others tread on hot iron and swallow flaming liquor. There was a genius in the California mines who made a national repute by biting through six pies at once on a wager. But this conquering man of jaw met his Waterloo when some wretch inserted a tin plate between the layers. England, which produced Shakespeare, also produced the phenomenon who drew and etched admirably with his toes. *Punch* tells us of a gentleman who thrilled society by giving his mind to the tie of his neckerchief. We have often seen an ephemeral reputation made by writing for the newspapers, and have even known a very few cases in which people were distinguished for quiet, unostentatious usefulness.

"It was reserved for the Golden State to make a peculiar merit of a man's arrival here within a certain time. If he was fortunate enough to cross the boundary or touch the shore before the last minute of the last hour of the last day of 1849, he is a Pioneer, entitled to honor as such, and especially entitled to a handsome notice in the newspapers when he dies, under the attractive caption of 'Death of a Forty-Niner,' or 'Another Pioneer Gone,' or, more succinct and pathetically suggestive, 'Passing Away.' If, in addition to the felicity of reaching California just when he did, he is banded in a society composed of men like himself, he will enjoy—if a *caput mortuum* can enjoy anything—

the proud satisfaction of having his virtues rehearsed in a preamble and resolutions, a copy of which will be duly forwarded to his family, if he have one; and he may even be followed to Lone Mountain by a procession of his late associates, wearing white gloves and gold or silver effigies of the grizzly bear, dear to every Pioneer, in rosettes upon their black coats. Thus an accident in a man's life is made a source of distinction above the multitude who toil and strive around him. And here we are reminded on what narrow contingencies greatness often depends. Had a fog delayed one hour outside the Heads the ship in which our Pioneer arrived—had one of the oxen which drew his wagon 'across the plains' given out just before he reached the State line, and caused him to camp beyond it one night more than he expected, his arrival might have been in 1850, instead of 1849, and he would thus have remained one of the unhonored mob. We knew one poor fellow who missed his opportunity by being detained at Valparaiso, for some unconventional excess of high spirits, repugnant to local prejudice and law, until after his ship had sailed for California.

"When we reflect how few out of the million can achieve distinction in any way, although the longing for it is so nearly universal, it seems a peculiarly happy circumstance that the California hegira afforded so many a chance to rise by a chronological accident. Byron says:

> 'Tis pleasant, sure to see one's name in print;
> A book's a book, although there's nothing in't.

And so the honor worn by our 'Pioneers of 'Forty-nine,' although so fortuitous and unpremeditated, is something to exult in and to be jealously guarded. Men who obtained it by perilous consumption of ligaminous and pachydermatous diet, by reckless expenditure of two Spanish reals on a stimulating beverage, by couching on poles and sand-beds, and by rigidly eschewing 'boiled shirts' until woman, like an angel, came to sew on the buttons, are entitled to a monopoly of their hard-earned glory. Yet there are envious people, who arrived here in the first minute of the first hour of the first day of 1850, who presume to dispute for the title of pioneer with these veterans! They even insist that the society founded by their illustrious predecessors shall be opened to them as equals —that the period to be known as the New Argonautic in the far future, to be sung as Virgil sung the arrival of Æneas in Italy, shall be extended by a whole twelvemonth, so as to admit to fame the tardy multitude who followed on the heels of their betters. Forbid it, spirits of adventure and romance! Forbid it, ghosts of Yerba Buena! Forbid it, ye noble army of canvas-backed heroes, wherever ye may be, in the flesh or out of it, who smoked together over the camp fires of 'Forty-nine, and dug deep for the glittering ore.

"There is a class of pioneers who put in no chronological claims to distinction, who have come here at various times during the last hundred years, and are still coming, who are content to work without special recognition, to do all the good they can without making a fuss about it, and to die without a newspaper notice or society resolution. These men are not concerned in this ungracious rivalry, and these men we do not address. Whether they came in one year or another, and whether anybody knows or cares when they came, is nothing to them. When we find people so indifferent to the noblest passion of the race, it is the best to let them toil on in their unnoticed way. Like the coral insects in the sea, they may, however, be building monuments, that will rise and speak for them when they are gone where dates are unknown and where fame is not."

The old resident who will stand to-day on the corner of Montgomery and Sacramento streets, or even at the corner of Leidesdorff, and look to the corner of Sansome, can hardly realize that Dall & Austin's store was no farther down Sacramento street than the northeast corner of Sansome. It used to seem a long way across the water to their store, standing on the little pier which was the commencement of Sansome, at the corner of Sacramento; and, when one had walked the length of Howison's Pier (now Sacramento street) to Hoff's store, on its extreme end, at the corner of Battery street, he seemed well on the way to Contra Costa. Many people cannot remember the appearance or position of the buildings as they stood in '49 and '50, unless refreshed by verbal description, or some lithograph of that time. It would be very interesting to look over a collection of all the old lithographs that have been made in the last twenty-four years. Some of the houses of '49 are standing exactly where they were originally built, and some have been moved to new locations.

The two-story wooden house on California street, north side, corner of the alley just above Kearny street, was built in 1849 by Dr. Jones, who may be remembered by the old residents. The doctor was an eccentric individual. He wore a long, velvet-lined voluminous cloak, with the air of a Spanish Grandee. It was said in those days, that the doctor had more gold-dust than any man in California. Those who knew him most intimately, used to tell a story of his spreading sheets over the floor of his sleeping apartment, pouring his gold-dust upon them, and walking upon it, pushing his feet through it, taking it up in his hands, and pouring it upon his head and shoulders, and rolling in it —performing Jupiter and Danæ, with Dr. Jones in both characters. During his sprees, and the doctor was often under the influence, he was fond of indulging in great absurdities. The doctor sold at one sale seventy-one lots, and liberally treated his friends at " Our House," on Washington street, just above Dunbar's Alley. Dr. Wallace purchased and occupied for many years the Dr. Jones house.

"Our House" was kept by Peter Sherrebeck, on the lower portion of the fifty-vara lot on the southeast corner of Washington and Kearny streets, the same formerly occupied by the El Dorado, now by the Hall of Records. There was no bar or counter for the dispensing of liquids. There was a table in the middle of the room, upon which the wines and spirits were placed, as in a private house. The name of Sherrebeck has been famous in our law courts in litigation for the property on Folsom and Second streets. Sherrebeck was a German, and came to San Francisco in 1846 or '47.

Montgomery street was not graded in the spring of '50. It was like any hill-side, with a gradual slope. Not that it was so very gradual either, for the western side was several feet higher than the eastern. Long Wharf, now Commercial street, opened into the eastern side of Montgomery, but was not then cut through the other side of it, as it now is, to Kearny. A large wooden building, with a very high, broad roof, the eaves of which projected over the benches, ranged against the side wall on Montgomery street, now the northwest corner of Commercial street. The front of this house faced the south, and on these benches sat or lounged Mexicans and Chilenos, in their native costumes, rolling up cigarettes, and smoking philosophically over their losses—for the building was used on the lower floor as a gambling saloon. A large American flag was displayed over the door ; strains of music—good music, too—floated upon the air; crowds of men of many nations were passing in and out. Within, many tables were spread with games: faro, monte, roulette, chuck-a-luck, etc., around which men were standing as closely as possible—betting, winning and losing, as quietly and earnestly as typos setting up copy. The music of the band, the tinkle of the dealers' bells, calling the waiters for drinks and cigars, and the subdued click of ivory checks, and clink of coin, went on incessantly, but a man's voice was rarely heard. The players reached out their stakes, laying them upon the card on which they wished to bet, or, if it were beyond their reach, handed it to some one to place for them, indicating by a simple monosyllable, spoken scarcely above a whisper, the card whereon to place it. The dealer sat, with unmoved features, until all had staked their money, and, with a nod, dealt the chances.

The scenes were just the same in the "Tontine," opposite, on the corner of Long Wharf, in the Bella Union, La Sociedad, El Dorado, The Empire, Parker House, Veranda, and all the gambling saloons. Those upon the Plaza were more elegantly furnished and decorated; longer, and more gaily appointed bars, flanked by great mirrors, pictures, glass and silverware. Cosmopolitan crowds flocked to the counter and around the tables, and in and out of the many entrances; the air was heavy with the odor of burning slow-match, or Chinese punk, for cigar lights, lying smoking in little miniature junks, at convenient distances, along the far-stretching bar; and incessant was the chink of golden ounces and Mexican dollars in the hands of the players at every table.

It was easy to tell the habitual gamblers, by the way they slid so skillfully, from hand to hand, the rolls of coin, smoothly and swiftly, with unerring certainty—pulling out the cylindrical piles, and gliding them again together, like little telescopes. Crowds of men, who never gambled a dollar in all their lives, came, led by curiosity, to pass the time and hear the music, which was well worth listening to. Everybody went there—for homes, reading-rooms and good society were rare in San Francisco at that time.

The building which we have mentioned as standing on the place now known as the northwest corner of Commercial and Montgomery streets, was in 1848, and previously, the Hudson Bay Company's House. It was a large wooden structure, two and a half stories, with a high, sloping roof, facing the south. In 1852, some laborers, digging a sewer in Commercial street, came upon a long, narrow wooden box, which, on the removal of the earth, proved to be a coffin. The awed workmen brushed the loose earth away from the oval glass, revealing, with ghastly distinctness, the grayish-white face of the dead. Singularly enough, the brow, the eyelids, nostrils, lips—all the features—retained their form, calm and peaceful, while, to the gazer's eyes, a sudden fancy seemed to catch upon the dead man's face—a look of sad remonstrance with the pressing throng's sacrilegious stare of vulgar curiosity, intruding even on the grave of the long-buried dead.

Crowds of people came to look; to turn away, wondering who this long-buried, silent sleeper, thus suddenly revisiting the glimpses of the moon, could be; how his grave happened to be there, exactly in the centre of that noisy, populous thoroughfare, resounding with the croupier's vociferous "*Rouge perd et la couleur!*" the ceaseless clink of coin at lansquenet; the gay music of instrumental bands in the gambling saloons; laughter, song and imprecations, and the never-ceasing tread of eager and excited men, all unconscious of the silent form beneath their feet.

Among all the curious gazers, none knew those wonderfully preserved features, once so familiar to many—so dear, surely, to some. Who could explain this mystery? At last, Mr. Bond, the confidential secretary of Wm. D. M. Howard, came that way, and he knew that the ground was formerly the garden of the house occupied by Wm. A. Rae, agent of the Hudson Bay Company, who rashly ended his life in 1846, and was buried in the then peaceful garden spot, where he had so long slept unmolested.

CHAPTER II.

The Custom House stood on the corner of California and Montgomery streets. It was built by Wm. H. Davis, in October, 1849. The stairs were on the outside, ending at each story, across which ran a veranda, or broad balcony. Collier was the Collector of the Port in 1849–'50, and Jesse D. Carr was the Deputy Collector. This building was built of brick, four stories in height, and the wood-work front painted white.

Kendig & Wainwright occupied the next building adjoining north. Wells, Fargo & Co's offices now stand on the ground where these buildings stood. Wainwright afterwards took a store on Montgomery, between Clay street and what is now Merchant street; and his auction advertisements in the *Alta California* of that day informed the people that they could lighter goods directly from the back doors of his salerooms to the steamers, quite an inducement to those wishing to save drayage, which was no small item in the account of large purchasers.

T. J. Poulterer's auction store was on the northwest corner of California and Montgomery, in Edward Vischer's building; the spot where W. H. Davies built the Custom House, in October, '49, just where Wells, Fargo & Co's banking house now stands. Sam. Gower was with Mr. Poulterer then, and they paid twenty-five hundred dollars per month rent for their store, and rented the "up-stairs" to Mr. Crane, of the *Courier* newspaper, for one thousand dollars per month. Many of our old residents will remember Mr. Gower; he was a native of Austria, a gentleman of the most agreeable manners and person—accomplished in music, languages, literature and mercantile affairs. Many years have gone since Mr. Gower left California, but his face would be very welcome should he return to meet the men of '50.

On the south side of California street, where Stevenson's building now stands, were some little wooden structures, where Capt. Folsom, Q. M. U. S. A., had his offices. Capt. Folsom had purchased the Leidesdorff estate, and it was here the Leidesdorff House stood in 1849. It did not stand on the street line, but diagonally, like the *Casa Grande*, built by Mr. Richardson, on Dupont street, between Clay and Washington, and Wm. H. Davis' house, near the corner of Stockton and Jackson. The road to the Presidio was along this line, upon which the houses stood.

On California street, above Montgomery, in 1849, the tents were pitched in the middle of the street, anywhere the dwellers chose, and interspersed with boxes, and bales of goods, and piles of lumber. There was an open space, about where Mars' assay office now stands, on California street, through which one could pass behind the Custom House and adjoining stores, and come out upon Montgomery street, where Bullock & Jones now have their place of business. Edward Vischer, Esq., the author and artist of "The Old Missions of California," lived in a cottage on this spot, accessible from either street. Mr. Meacham also lived in his house near Mr. Vischer's. Subsequently, Rowe, the pioneer of ring amusements, had on this spot the Olympic Circus.

Mr. Rowe went from California to Australia, where he was very successful. On his return, he brought $95,000 in sovereigns. He also brought a beautiful design, in gold—a group emblematical of equine sports—as a gift for Wm. D. M. Howard, who, with his proverbial generosity, had aided Mr. Rowe in times gone by. The costly token was exhibited in a jeweler's window on Montgomery street at the time. We are glad to record this evidence of gratitude, wishing ourselves possessed of an amount equal to that never returned by those indebted to the most generous of California's pioneers.

The old road, or path, to the Mission Dolores in '49 or '50 was the same as had been used for eighty years prior to the gold discovery—a winding way among the sand-hills and chaparral, keeping to the level, solid ground, and avoiding the deep, toilsome sand. Col. Hays' house was the half-way stopping-place between the city and the Mission. At the Mission, Bob Ridley and C. V. Stuart kept the Mansion House, part of the old Mission building, adjoining the church, just as it stands to-day. The long rail of the veranda was the hitching-post for the saddle-horses; a vehicle was rather a curiosity until the plank-road was constructed. In the afternoon, the horses stood thick and close, like a cavalry halt, at Bob Ridley's door. Within, milk-punch was always plentiful, like the lager of later, degenerate years. Nearly all the residents of San Francisco in those days rode horseback, used the Mexican saddle and all the jingling accoutrements; wore the vicuna hat, or broad-brimmed glazed *sombrero*, and the comfortable, convenient, protecting *serapa*. The new comers were pleased with *costume de la Pais*—its novelty and its easy negligence. Everybody was cordial, prosperous and happy.

We were out at the Mission one warm, pleasant Sunday morning, not long ago, sitting upon a bench in front of the old Mansion House. We closed our eyes to shut out the street-car; the blocks of modern buildings; *cottages orneé;* the fashionable, scant, nipped-looking coats and skin-tight pants of the scores of men continually passing; the ridiculous head-gear and swollen, puffed-out paniers of the gentler sex. As we sat with closed eyes, the atmosphere was just the same upon our cheek, just as refreshing to our lungs, had precisely the same somnolent effect stealing over our senses. Sleep used to be called the California fever, before the gold discovery, and we fell into a reverie of the past. We heard the jingling spurs, we saw the gay, silver-mounted bridles, the fancy saddles, the rushing horse and rider, dashing up at full speed directly at us, sitting upon the veranda, seemingly intent upon riding us down madly; but, just as we were springing in consternation from our seat, the horse was upon his haunches—there was a crunching of hoofs upon the gravel, a confused rattling of spurs, snorting, champing of the cruel Mexican bit—a cloud of dust over all—and, when we had collected our startled ideas sufficiently to feel assured we were not beneath the horse's hoofs, we saw the dismounted *caballero* taking from the pommel the long-coiled *riata* to "hitch" his steed, preparatory to imbibing one of Bob Ridley's nourishing milk-punches. It was trying to the newcomer's nerves to learn the California style of riding up to dismount—to sit quietly and see horse and rider dashing at full speed directly for you, as if both were bent upon dashing through the wall of the house, nor abating in the least their speed until within five feet of you, then stopped with a shock—sudden as if struck by lightning. We sat upon the old bench, enjoying the warm sun and the same delightful atmosphere we breathed twenty-odd years ago, shutting our eyes to the sights of to-day, and looking back upon the memories—the men we saw when first we knew the Mission Dolores: El Señores Valencia, Noe, Guerrero, De Haro, Bernal and Charley Brown, who came there in 1829; Messrs. Denniston and Nuttman, of Stevenson's Regiment, and Jack Powers, always well mounted, and dashing along to show the merits of his nag. Jack Powers! with black beard and flowing hair—his glittering, restless, omnivagant eye—the worst we ever looked upon in any living creature—a fascinating terror—sure index of the devil, time eventually proved him to be.

Our reverie, so long and deep, is broken. A procession of Holy Fathers, in sacerdotal robes and church insignia! What saint's day is this? How the sight of their bowed heads, slow, solemn step and chant, with burning candles, brings back the olden days. We had thought this custom unobserved of late in our busy city neighborhood. In the true spirit of old-time respect, we rise to lift our hat and stand with head bowed and uncovered while they pass. It seems—eh? how confusing—they never used to shake such a harsh bell as that! My head is—well, sure enough, I was asleep!—blinking in the sunlight. I now discern a man gesticulating violently to me. 'Tis he, ringing the harsh, discordant bell that swept away the Holy Fathers—rudely, with lightning speed! dragging me back, over more than twenty years of life's uneven road—away from the vesper-bells, the soft evening air, the low, sweet music of her voice, breathing *la lengua de los angeles*, to ——
"All aboard, now, for the city!" Harsh and discordant clash these selfish days against the memory of those halcyon hours. Alas! why could we not still dream?

There was another road, or path, for horsemen and pedestrians, by which one might reach the old Mission track. It was along Kearny, turning by Caryll's stable, up Bush street to the hill, where a sharp turn brought you before the house built by Judge Burritt—the same since occupied by Lucien Hermann, and until quite recently by Dr. A. J. Bowie. As this pretty cottage now stands, on the corner of Sutter and Stockton, flanked by regular sidewalks, the lofty synagogue towering above it, and blocks of houses, as far as the eye can see in every direction, it does not give the passer-by that pleasurable start of emotion experienced by him who, winding his way among the desert of sandhills and chaparral twenty-two years ago, came suddenly upon the bright, new, stylish residence—its nicely curtained, spotless windows, perfect roof, and finished chimneys, neat porch, veranda, paths and door-way, lying in the warm sunlight, nestling among the cheerless sandhills, like a sweet bit of our old home spirited across the continent by fairies' wand, and softly dropped among the unsightly huts and fragile tenements in which we lived—a gentle admonition that we might give a little less of heart and soul to money, and a little more to comfort, beauty and utility. He who had been turned on a reflective vein by this unexpected vision of a home in the wilderness, then traveled down the line of Stockton across Sutter, Post, Geary and O'Farrell, his horse's hoofs noiseless, plunging at every step knee-deep in unresisting sand; saddle and bridle trappings jingling, a clink of spurs, and the deep breathing of the horse; saddle-leather creaking with every step, but not a sound of hoof in the soft, sinking sand, more than a phantom horse—on, past O'Farrell to Ellis, around Mr. John Sullivan's cottage into St. Ann's Valley, skirting the gardens and hot-houses—the remnant of which still remains on Eddy, between Powell and Mason—where the path wound in and out among sand mounds and ridges, piled up like dirty snow-drifts, with here and there a charcoal-burner's hut, and clumps of scrub-oaks, until he came to Col. Thomas Hayes' house, where it was customary to stop awhile, for there were always many there, chatting, while their horses rested. This long, white house stood diagonally with the Mission road, in a little, open space, where ground was firmer than the deep sand outside the circle of small trees and shrubs surrounding it—a spot where one would naturally halt to rest, were there no hospitable roof upon it. A little further on, a turn to the right, brought the traveler on the old Mission road, where soon he crossed a little, shallow, slow, but limpid brook, edged by willows, running across the Harmen tract, and down MacClaren's lane toward Mission Creek. The same brook's course, diverted, now runs through Woodward's Gardens, refreshing the pelicans and pink-billed swans. Past this stream, the rider turned diagonally across the block now bounded by Mission and Center streets, and halted at the Mansion House.

On the old Mission road, many years ago—twenty or more—was a little roadside public-house, called "The Grizzly." We do not remember its precise location, but it was very near the turn of the road, just before you came (going Mission-ward) to the cottages of R. C. Page, C. R. Peters and E. H. Parker. "The Grizzly" stood a little way from the road, on the north side, and surrounded by scrub-oaks. A little brown bear—what is known as the cinnamon bear—was chained to the trunk of one of these oak trees, and whenever we passed there, which was almost every day, for years, the bear was leaning forward to the full stretch of his chain, treading from side to side, with that peculiar rocking step and swaying movement of caged wild beasts. He must have been quiet at some time, of course, but we never saw him when not treading his incessant step. We often halted there, lingering awhile, to see if he would not be quiet; but his monotonous and never ceasing movement so disquieted, and in a certain indescribable way, confused our nerve and vision, that we always gave it up.

We never knew whether this cinnamon bruin was the successor to some genuine grizzly cub, the possession of which induced its owner to build and name the inn, under the impression that *symposiac* profits would accrue from visitors curious to see the ursine captive; or whether, after building this traveler's retreat, his patronymic project failed by sheer inability to find a grizzly, forcing him to compromise with the cinnamon. But, most certainly the name upon the signboard was a misnomer, if the chained specimen of the *genus ursus cinnamominus* were offered as an adjunct corroboration.

CHAPTER III.

PIOCHE & BAYERQUE had their store on the north side of Clay street, just below Kearny. Davidson's bank was just below them. Then came Bennett & Kirby's store; William Hobourg was a partner in their house. Bagley & Sinton were adjoining. Cross, Hobson & Co. were opposite. The Adelphi Theater was about half way between Kearny and Montgomery streets, on the south side of Clay, and was used for theatrical performances, concerts, balls, etc. W. H. Lyon kept the bar of the theater. Riddle & Co's auction store was not built on the corner of Clay and Montgomery until July or August, 1850. Etting Mickle's store was on the north side of Clay, between Montgomery and Leidesdorff. Selim and Fred. Woodworth's store was just at the water's edge, on the north side of Clay. Below, on the wharf, were the stores of J. J. Chariteau, Simmons, Hutchinson & Co., F. Vassault, and the office of the Sacramento steamers. Fay, Pierce & Willis were commission merchants on the corner of Clay and Montgomery.

Jno. B. Corrigan was a commission merchant on Clay street wharf. Mr. Corrigan went to Washoe in the earliest days of silver mining, and died there. He was a noble-hearted, genial man, and his memory is kindly cherished in the hearts of all who knew him.

Moorhead, Whitehead & Waddington were at the foot of Clay street. This was a Valparaiso firm, doing business in San Francisco, dealing in flour by the cargo. Hochkofler & Tenequel were near by. Mr. Hochkofler came from Valpariso with a member of the firm of Morehead, Whitehead & Waddington, *via* Panama, and arrived here on the sixth of June, 1850, on board the steam-propeller *Columbus*, Capt. Peck.

Capt. Frank Eldredge, Chas. Peck (of Stevenson's Regiment), Mr. Beck (Beck & Elam), Jno. F. Osgood, James George, Capt. Treadwell, Capt. Chadwick, Messrs. Barry & Patten, Theo. Nash, Mr. Dewey, John Corson, James Howard, John Ling, Dr. Smiley, Sawyer & Chapin, and many others whose names we cannot now recall, were passengers on the same steamer.

We remember as vividly as if it were but yesterday the arrival of the *Columbus*. In those days there were few wharves for the vessels to swing alongside of, so they dropped anchor out in the stream, where they were surrounded by boats to convey passengers and baggage ashore. One new comer by the *Columbus* had a fine bunch of pine-apples, purchased at San Blas for *un peso*, and carefully preserved for the San Francisco market. He had hardly set foot on Montgomery street, when a man hailed him with, "D'ye want to sell them?" "Well, yes!" "How much?" The amateur importer of tropical fruits looked at his questioner, and, with the air of a man who was venturing on an absurdity which would never be entertained for one moment, said— "Well, you may have them for ten dollars!" "Here's your money!" said the man, clutching the pine-apples, and thrusting a ten dollar piece into the hand of the astonished individual, who, for a moment, could not realize that it was his first negotiation on the shores of his adopted home, and not a joke. He was not long in doubt, however. Two or three men had stopped on the street to look at the tempting fruit while the bargain was being made. One of them said to the purchaser, "How many are there?" "Six!" "Want to sell 'em?" "No!" "Will yer sell three of 'em?" "Yes!" "*Quanto?*" "Fifteen dollars!" "Here's your *dinero*," said the man, handing over three five-dollar pieces.

and walking off like one greatly pleased with his purchase. The *Columbus* passenger was observed to walk away with that peculiar expression of countenance noticeable in new students of Euclid.

Ogden & Haynes were commission merchants on Clay street wharf. They had ships from China. We remember the arrival of the *Fanny Major* from China, with a cargo of teas, shawls, silks, fancy furniture, etc. Billy Buckler, of Baltimore, had goods on the vessel, and on her arrival, he came ashore with a couple of grotesque stoneware images under his arm, and brought them up to Barry & Patten, just for a joke with his old friends. They received them, drank the health of the donor, and placed them behind their counter, where they stand to-day, old and time-honored citizens, though ineligible for the Association of Pioneers. Ogden & Haynes were liberal, public-spirited men, without fuss or ostentation. Mr. Haynes has gone to the reward of all good men. Mr. Ogden is still with us; and if there be any change in his personal appearance as we knew him twenty-three years ago, our eyes fail to detect it.

It is a pleasure to observe any man through nearly a quarter of a century's vicissitudes and temptations, in a city where cosmopolitan allurements have gathered in force, and to note, through all, no loss of that refinement of taste and feeling; no blunting of that æsthetic appreciation, the possession of which preserves the mind, even as pure air and temperance does the body. Mr. Ogden is a facile writer, and often contributes to the newspapers of San Francisco. Mr. John Haynes, a brother of the late Thomas Haynes, Mr. Ogden's former partner, is a resident of San Francisco, having arrived here on the steamer *Columbus*, June 6th, 1850.

The Hon. John W. Dwinelle and his brother, the Hon. Samuel H. Dwinelle, were counsellors-at-law in Cross, Hobson & Co's building on Clay street, nearly opposite Bagley & Sinton's store. S. H. Dwinelle is now the Judge of the Fifteenth District Court, and esteemed by the members of the bar of California as one of the best lawyers and most upright Judges in the State. J. W. Dwinelle is one of the ablest members of the bar, a Regent of the University of California, and as a conversationalist the peer of Dr. A. J. Bowie, Judge Hoffman, or the late Hon. Mr. De la Torre, U. S. District Attorney for California.

Cross, Hobson & Co. afterwards removed to the large corrugated-iron warehouse on Sansome street, between Jackson and Pacific, where

William Hooper also had an office. We never pass this old iron store without recalling (as we look at the broad loft door, just above the main entrance on Sansome street) a tragic occurrence which happened there in 1851. Pedro, the porter of the store, was standing at the open doorway of the loft, speaking to some one on the walk below, when leaning forward to hear more distinctly, he fell out, struck upon his head, and died instantaneously. Pedro was a native of Manila; a pleasant, faithful servant, who had the regard of all who knew him.

Woodworth & Morris were shipping and commission-merchants on Clay street wharf. Selim E. Woodworth (subsequently Commodore Woodworth, U. S. N.) was the senior member of this firm. Fred. A. Woodworth, a younger brother, was in the same house. Selim arrived in San Francisco in the winter of 1846–7, and built the first house ever erected upon a "water-lot" in San Francisco. Some time after his arrival, news reached the city of a party of emigrants dying of starvation on the mountain trail to California, and he immediately started with a party to their rescue, and succeeded in saving many of them, although several had died, and the living, when found by Mr. Woodworth's party, were eating the dead bodies of their unfortunate companions. All through his life in California, Selim Woodworth was foremost in acts of charity, and in the protection of life and property, or the swift punishment of outlaws and criminals. He was small in stature, but had the bravery and spirit of a giant, never to be intimidated either by threats or force of arms. To his courage and determination San Francisco owes more than to any other man its release from the criminals that infested it in the early days. Both Selim and Fred. Woodworth made their abode–at their store in the primitive times, and in their family residence in after years—extremely pleasant to their umerous friends, who remember with a sad pleasure the happy hours passed in the hospitable home from which the two brothers have gone forth forever.

CHAPTER IV.

The Fuller House—not a hotel, but the home of the Fuller family—was about a hundred feet east of the eastern line of Webb street, considerably nearer to California street than Sacramento street. The Fuller estate was the Kearny street half of the block bounded by Kearny, California, Montgomery and Sacramento streets. P. B. Hewlett, a captain in Stevenson's regiment, bought some property in Webb street, west side, and built a house there. It was a kind of semi-hotel and semi-boarding-house, conducted by a very pretty widow lady. This house was quiet and comfortable; the table and sleeping arrangements far in advance of the average in 1850. Col. Whiting, F. H. Price, M. Jazynsky, Barry & Patten, and Col. Thompson boarded there. Capt. Argyras, the Greek gentleman who was the owner of the celebrated yacht *Northern Light*, also boarded there. This yacht was in 1847–8–9 the fancy boat of Boston. Argyras sailed on an expedition, more for pleasure than business; but his plans were frustrated by the loss of his yacht in the Straits of Magellan. Argyras was an educated, refined and honorable gentleman. He died in San Francisco about ten years since. James Ward built a cottage on this block, nearer to Montgomery street. Mrs. Meacham afterwards kept it as a boarding-house. We remember her house, for the reason that an acquaintance obtained quarters there for himself, wife and two children for three hundred dollars per week.

Capt. Hewlett lived on Montgomery, beyond Broadway, high up, toward the telegraph station. He had a very comfortable little snuggery; two stories and weather proof, as far as rain was concerned; an enclosure for his wood-pile and well-house, and it may here be mentioned that a well of water was a nice thing to have in those days, when water was a "bit" per bucket.

Don Pedro, as we used to call Capt. Hewlett, although his name was Palmer B. Hewlett, always had several friends living with him. He made a pretense of charging them for board, but it was only to have the pleasure of their company, and relieve them of any sense of obligation—a very transparent sham—not beginning to reimburse him for the outlay of their accommodation. But, hospitable Don Pedro vowed he was a manager, and knew how to keep house. On the morning of the fourteenth of June, 1850, as the company were lingering over breakfast, some one ran down the steep hillside past the house, crying "Fire!" All sprang up from the table, and ran to the edge of the little ravine in which the house stood. A high rising cloud of smoke and a little fire were seen somewhere near Kearny street, beyond the Plaza. Some new comers in the party observed the fire indifferently, and were turning back to the house, but Don Pedro, who had been here at all the conflagrations, said, with a meaning smile, "You'd better be looking after your baggage, if it's in the city." The person addressed answered, "Oh, it cannot reach the place where our trunks are—in Riddle's store on Sacramento street, below Montgomery." "If you don't hurry, the fire will be there before you are," said Don Pedro, with such evident earnestness that his friend started. Two or three of the party went with him. As they descended the hill, they kept watch of the fire's progress, and, before they had passed Pacific street, the flames were rushing on like a train of powder. The party commenced running, nor abated their pace until they reached the store of Riddle & Eaton, on Sacramento street, two doors west of Leidesdorff. The block was on fire at the corner of Montgomery when they passed it. They rushed up stairs to secure their trunks, which were in the upper story; and, before they descended to the street, the roof of the building was in full blaze. They saved their trunks, but they dared not wait to collect some other articles belonging to them. This experience, however, was sufficient to convince them of Don Pedro's wisdom in regard to San Francisco conflagrations. The structures in those days were of the slightest and most inflammable materials; the rooms lined with cloth and paper,—buildings which, after standing a few weeks in this atmosphere, became tinder—food for the first spark. If a fire broke out, this dry material burned so suddenly and furiously, that, though the air were dead calm, the wind soon rushed in, sweeping all in its path.

The Bella Union (temple of chance) was on the Plaza, Washington street side, just above Kearny, and was, in the days of '49 and '50, thronged with men playing against the various games from about eleven o'clock in the morning until daylight the next morning. The same motley crowd as frequented the Parker House, Empire, El Dorado, etc., were to be seen here. There used to be a quintette of Mexican musicians, who came here at night to perform. There were two harps, one large and the other very small, two guitars, and one flute.

The musicians were dressed in the Mexican costume (which, however, was nothing very noticeable at that time, as many of their auditors were in the same style of dress), and were quiet, modest looking men, with contented, amiable faces. They used to walk in among the throng of people, along to the upper end of the room, take their seats, and with scarcely any preamble or discussion, commence their instrumentation. They had played so much together, and were so similar, seemingly, in disposition—calm, confident and happy—that their ten hands moved as if guided by one mind; rising and falling in perfect unison—the harmony so sweet, and just strange enough in its tones, from the novelty in the selection of instruments, to give it a peculiar fascination for ears always accustomed to the orthodox and time-honored vehicles of music used in quintette instrumentation.

Their *repertoire* contained the popular waltzes and dances of the time, and many weird, curious airs of old Spain, sad refrains and amorous *Lieder ohne worte*; the listener knew, intuitively, though he heard the music without the words, that the same sounds had, with words, centuries ago, floated on the moonlit night in old Seville, beneath the iron-latticed balconies where lovely señoritas listened with bated breath, and thrilled with sympathetic recognition.

In the Bella Union at that time might have been seen a man about fifty years of age, rather above the medium height, with a refined, intellectual and rather sad face; forehead, high, broad and white; gray, neatly combed and rather long hair; white cravat and black suit. This individual presided with quiet and unruffled dignity at the very interesting but baffling enigma known as "Faro"—*genus felis tigris*.

The courteous gravity with which he witnessed the fluctuations of the game and the undisturbed serenity of his benign features, through heavy loss or high success, was always a study for the physiognomist and observer of human nature.

One afternoon, a grave looking man, and clerical in appearance, stopped in his stroll through the crowded saloon—all the games were very busy that afternoon—in front of the closely surrounded table, where sat, dealing the cards, he, so long our study. So much absorbed was he in the complication of the stakes, piled up so heavily, on, and between, and at the corners of every card on the green cloth, that he never once raised his eyes higher than the hands that placed the stacks of coin, or "chips" in their respective places.

Now, the deal being out, and a fresh shuffle and cut finished, and the pack slid within the little silver box, (bigger with fate than ever was Pandora's), our urbane friend leaned back for a moment in his chair, awaiting the movements of the players.

Happening to raise his eyes, he looked upon the clerical-looking man, whose earnest gaze had, from the moment of his halt at the table, been fixed upon the face of the all-unconscious dealer. A keen observer might have detected a slight start, and sudden but faint flush upon the face of the grave arbiter of chance; but it was scarcely discernable, and the next moment the face was placid and self-possessed as usual. When the deal was finished, the dealer rang a bell which stood always at his hand, and spoke quietly to the attendant servant, who quickly disappeared, and soon returned with a pale, impassible-faced man, of slight, delicate figure, and hands thin, small, blue-veined and white, as those of a lady. Without any communication save a direct glance into the eyes of the retiring dealer, he sat down, took from a drawer in the table a new pack of cards, divested them of their cover, then for a moment his facile fingers slid them in and out, without a single ruffle or catch; smooth, sure, and with regular exactness, slapped the well-shuffled pack upon the table, in front of his nearest right-hand neighbor, who cut them, and the game proceeded as usual. Meantime, he who had left the chair walked leisurely out of the room to the open plaza, first giving a glance to the clerical-looking man, and an indication of the head towards the door. In a moment the two were engaged in close and earnest conversation, which lasted some considerable time. The purport of that conference was never known; but many of the "Sports" from Alabama and Mississippi surmised its nature, as they had known both gentlemen as eloquent preachers in the Methodist Church South.

CHAPTER V.

Many of our readers will remember H——n, a member of the Pioneer Association. He was an enigma to everybody during the last years of his life. In the early days, from '49 to '53, he was, like the majority of Californians, engaged in any kind of business or speculation offering a profit—whether real estate or commission, brokerage or what not. As those days for sudden and richly remunerative operations passed away, and business settled itself into the grooves and confines of ordinary times and places, H——n also conformed to the changed condition of circumstances in business, by a corresponding formality in his attire. Always scrupulously neat in dress, and, even in the most careless, red-shirt, unkempt period of pioneer days, he was never to be seen without a certain jaunty style, becoming in its very negligence. But, when the city assumed the ways of older cities, when it was blessed by the coming of wives, mothers, sisters, and little ones, and social relations were established, then H——n donned the formal suit of black—the black, high-crowned hat, the dainty dress-boots, and faultless gloves of *mode* color. His clothes were always the perfection of fit and style,— would have passed at Poole's in London, or Wyman & Derby's in New York; his hair and beard were ever trimmed and dressed with the utmost care; his figure was tall, erect and elegant; his waist slender, and his shoulders well proportioned. At a certain hour in the afternoon he appeared on Montgomery street, promenading its length for an hour or so, noticeable for his gait, dress, and old-beau, courtier deportment. Those who did not know him supposed him to be a stranger, taking a look at San Francisco. Citizens to whom his form was familiar, and who knew him only by sight, smiled, perhaps a little contemptuously, as his well-known figure passed. No one really knew him with sufficient intimacy to tell of his manner of life, his means of subsistence, his dwelling place, or where or how he passed the time, when not seen taking his regular afternoon promenade. He never failed to be present at all stated meetings of the Pioneer Association, at the parades, celebrations and funerals.

On Sunday morning he was at some one of the

churches, an attentive and devout worshiper. He was a man considerably past middle age, but remarkably youthful in appearance, manners and movement, making all due allowance for any artificial aid in producing or maintaining this impression, to which one might suspect he resorted. We remember once, during a chatty conversation in the Pioneer rooms, one of our party said, in reply to some remark, "That is the year and month when I was born—thirty-seven years ago!" "Ah, ha!" said H———n, in his quiet, unobtrusive and pleasant way. "You are a mere boy; a mere boy, sir! Why, in that month, and that year, I was at Niagara Falls on my wedding tour! Yes sir! on my wedding tour with my beautiful bride." Here he had leaned back in his chair, raised his eyes to the ceiling, and brought the tips of his fingers and thumbs together in the most gentle manner, like one forgetful of all around, musing over the long, dim years of the past. "Yes sir! yes, there are many members here who were born after my dear wife and children died; after the time when we were all living so happily together, just as so many are to-day, and as I supposed we were to live on together, happily and comfortably to old age. What a dream it seems—so long ago! Well, well! 'Life's but a dream!'" Suddenly recalled to his surroundings, he glanced uneasily about for a moment; arose, rubbed his gloved hands gently over the lappels of his neat coat; arranged his hat with exactness upon his carefully dressed hair; bowed with an air worthy of Sir Charles Grandison, and saying in his soft, courteous voice, "Good morning, gentlemen!" walked daintily away.

We believe H———n was an Englishman by birth, and came to the United States in infancy. We also believe that we once heard him state that he graduated at West Point, but chose a commercial life, in which for many years he was very successful. Certainly, his carriage and address had much in it to justify the belief that he might have been one of the cadets of West Point; for, with all due respect to the army officers of the past ten years, there was and is to-day, among all the remaining officers of the old *regime,* a distinguishing and unmistakable *ton,* a something which made the "button" a passport to all good society, an endorsement with all business men in pecuniary transactions; and we never yet knew one of them to abuse these privileges, or to be guilty of unbecoming conduct, in all the many years during which we have had constant and peculiar opportunities to know them.

To say that the object of our sketch had much in his deportment like an army officer of twenty years ago, is as high a compliment as we need pay his memory.

The vigor and elasticity apparent in H——n's carriage and movements was not assumed. We were one day in Thibault's office on Montgomery street, near Clay, and H——n was sitting near the desk, transacting some business. When it was concluded, he arose to go, and put his hand upon the hand-rail which ran down each side of the room, enclosing the different offices and desks. "Here's the gate!" said Mr. Thibault, politely rising to open it. "Thanks! don't trouble yourself," said H——, vaulting over the rail, before Mr. Thibault could carry out his his intention. "Well done!" said the astonished notary. "School-boy! eh?" H——n smiled, saying, as he walked away, "I don't feel anything of old age as yet, though 'tis many years since my school-boy days."

As the years rolled on, working their visible change in everybody and everything, they seemed to have granted immunity to our old friend. He came and went at the regular hour for his daily promenade, dressed with the same fastidious care, in clothes above reproach—hat, gloves and boots, hair and beard, a marvel of neatness. One afternoon, some one said, "I haven't seen H———n to-day,—didn't see him yesterday, either!" "Well, I hadn't noticed," said another. "He's always along the street, punctual as clock-work. I wonder where he is? —sick, perhaps!" and they walked on, forgetting all about the matter. On the third day of his absence from the street, the morning papers contained a notice of H———n's death. He had occupied a portion of the loft in a warehouse near the junction of Davis and California streets, where, known only to the immediate neighbors, he had been living and engaged in stuffing cushions for pews, coaches and carriages, making and renovating the coverings for hassocks and footstools. Here he had toiled and earned his daily bread, gaining by honorable industry the food and raiment for which his self-respect and a just pride would never let him beg, while life remained. Here he had lived alone, so many dreary days and years—no relative, friend, or companion—not even the cheering hopefulness of youth to encourage him with thoughts of brighter days, and the belief of prosperous times to come. There is something pathetically touching in the thought of this kind, brave old man working on so pluckily, even unto death, in the laudable struggle to be independent and respectable—to win the pittance that should enable him to come among his fellow-men in gentlemen's attire—equally presentable at any time, with any of them—to retain the position and outward semblance which had all through life been his; and with that praiseworthy ambition, fighting poverty and growing infirmity to the very last—a truer picture of the Argonaut of '49 than has often been presented, as the experience of many men can testify.

Those who were the first to enter the room where lay the remains of poor old H———n, saw upon one side of the room that which was so like him, so many years familiar to them—the neat and shapely coat, arranged upon some contrivance to keep its comely smoothness, just as if H———n himself, without his head, were in it. On a table, what seemed to be his head,—a wig, with every lock and parting so smooth and precise, so life-like and familiar, that it seemed as though one, looking at the front, must see the well-remembered face of H———n, instead of the wooden block they found. Across a chair his shirt was carefully laid, its neat bosom covered with a spread handkerchief; his other clothing carefully disposed—his gloves lying together, his boots standing with their heels in soldier fashion—everything like H———n; but when they turned to the bed, their eyes looked upon something they had never seen or known, —a white and hollow face, with sunken lips; the forehead high and pale, without one vestige of hair; but, strange incongruity! against the ghastly whiteness of its cheeks, and covering the fallen chin, a coal-black beard, precisely cut and trimmed, as if Death had, by one icy touch, made still more mysterious the man whose life was always an enigma.

CHAPTER VI.

In 1850, and for some time previous, Liedesdorff street was only half a street, a narrow levee, piled and capped, as a boundary for the tide-waters along the beach, where now the western line of the street runs from Clay to Sacramento, at which point the beach took a turn—a little *rincon* down to the corner of California and Sansome streets, thence sweeping to the corner, diagonally opposite, where stood Dewey & Heiser's store, built upon piles. The sidewalk in front of this store was reached at the corner, by steps, and under the store the tide ebbed and flowed. From the rear of this and all the stores between California and Pine streets, lighters could be loaded or discharged at tide-serving.

In June, 1850, we saw the surveyors, who were defining the boundaries for the foundations of the Tehama House, compelled to move tripods, theodolites and chains, or get wet feet in the advancing tide. Col. Folsom built the Tehama, or Jones' Hotel, the rendezvous of the army—Gen. Clark, Col. Ben. Beall, Lieut. Derby ("John Phœnix"), Cols. Andrews, Lendrum, Jones, Hamilton, Underhill, Capts. Hunt, Bonnycastle, Gibson, Whiting, Blake, Chandler, Ihrie, Gen. Allen, and in short, all the army officers of that day. Native Californians, and old *residentes* from the interior, always "put up" at the Tehama, because it was a wooden structure, spread out broad upon the ground, with spacious balconies on all sides, giving one a sense of security in case of Mother Earth being seized with a shiver. Apropos of earthquakes, we know people who have lived in San Francisco since 1829, and never yet knew a shock of sufficient severity to damage any well built house. The stores and warehouses which have been injured have either stood on made land, or have been constructed by incompetent builders.

The "Tehama" was noted for the cleanliness of its sleeping rooms and bedding. The single rooms were not, to be sure, large enough to swing cats in; but, as some wag said in answer to that, "Who wants to swing cats in his sleeping apartment?" It opened with *table d'hote* in good style; but subsequently that feature of the institution was changed, and Raphael opened a restaurant in the house, with public tables, and private rooms for families living in the hotel.

This house became, at last, one of the familiar sights, even to those who came long after its construction, standing as it did from 1850 to the time of its removal to make way for the Bank of California. The good-looking countenance of Geo. Washington Frink, the landlord, and the figure of John Durkin at the office desk, were almost as firm fixtures as the house itself. If you were hunting a visitor to the city, or an army or navy officer, you naturally went to the Tehama, and if John Durkin told you he was out, you immediately turned your steps to Barry & Patten's, on Montgomery street, where, if you did not find him, you sat down for five minutes, when he was sure to come in.

Looking among the old-time reminiscences upon Barry & Patten's walls, we find a small lithograph—a view of California street from the corner of Sansome, in 1849. Turning the little frame, we read upon its back, in the Hon. John W. Dwinelle's handwriting, "Photographed and retouched by Nahl, in 1868, from a drawing made in 1849, by William Cogswell, for John W. Dwinelle. Presented to Messrs. Barry & Patten, October, 1868, by John W. Dwinelle." The little sketch represents a boatman hauling his dory up the beach. Just above the water's edge, a man is sitting on some baggage, waiting the boatman's operations. Close by, another man is unloading a heavily laden mule—an every-day group along the beach in '49 and '50. On the right, in this little sketch, is a little one-story wooden building, upon the roof of which is the sign-board of S. H. Williams & Co., and over the door-way the sign "G. B. Post."

A rough board fence, with gate, extends from the outer end of this structure down the sloping beach into the water. On the south-west corner is a larger building, with the sign "Starkey, Janoin & Co." The perspective of the street shows irregular wooden buildings piles of lumber, and tents, which, above Montgomery, are standing in the middle of the street, promiscuously, as it rises the hill to Kearny street. Another lithograph upon the wall, close by, represents the stores and offices on the east side of Montgomery, south of Jackson; the first occupied by S. P. Dewey, real estate; Samuel Fleischacker, wholesale clothing; Pratt & Cole, attorneys and notaries, and Brooks, Sheppard & McCracken, attorneys; the next building, by H. Schroeder & Van Der Meden & Co., merchants; the next by J. B. Bidleman, shipping and commission merchant; the fourth by Theodore Payne & Co., auction and commission merchants. It was on the Jackson street corner of this block that packages of tobacco were used to make a sidewalk, it having been discovered one morning, that, in the mutability of California affairs, whole boxes of fine Virginia tobacco were cheaper than State of Maine pine boards. Theodore Payne was a warm-hearted, generous man, ever ready to aid the needy, a true friend and worthy citizen; and it pleases us here to say that his sons inherit the virtues of their father.

C. C. Richmond had his wholesale drug store just around the corner on Jackson, south side, below Montgomery. This store was on piles, and the sidewalk was raised several feet above the middle of the street, which was a shelving beach, covered with the tide "twice in twenty-four hours," if we may be allowed a "square" quotation. Sansome street was occupied with stores from the cliff at Broadway to the corner of Jackson, where it ended in the curve of the water line which swept up towards Washington, a little below Montgomery street, and approaching still nearer to Montgomery as it came to Clay street.

Beck & Elam were on Jackson street, south side, below Montgomery. Mr. Beck came to San Francisco as purser of the propeller *Columbus*.

He did not leave Panama as purser, but was elected to the office by the passengers, who found themselves—five hundred and twenty-four in number—at sea, aboard of a six hundred ton steamship, with no particular stem or stern to the discipline, whatever might be said of those portions of the ship's hull. Captain Peck was the ostensible commander—a very amiable man, who passed much of his time playing checkers, or draughts, with unconventional steerage passengers. Captain Peck was "as mild a mannered man" as you would wish to meet, but not one to be compared with Captain Bob Waterman, for having things in "shipshape and Bristol fashion." Mr. Beck was made to accept the office *nolens volens*, and he managed things very well. The five hundred and twenty-four passengers were five hundred and twenty-five when the steamer arrived in San Francisco, owing to an arrival among the lady passengers while at sea.

The clipper ship *Eclipse*, Captain Hamilton, came consigned to Beck & Elam; and we remember a gentleman, at a convivial entertainment, given in honor of her arrival, attempting to offer a sentiment, rather late in the dessert. "Gentlemen! I give you the shipper-clips—the clippy-sh—the—Gentlemen!! I give you the—

the slipper"—here he paused, steadied himself by the table-edge, bowed with great gravity, and said very slowly: "Gentlemen—I—give—you—the—ship—E—clipse, and her gallant cap'nhamilton." The last three words, "gallantcap'nhamilton," were too much for him, and he subsided.

Bullit & Patrick were on the corner of Jackson and Sansome streets; Coghill & Arrington were on the opposite corner; Christal, Cornan & Co. were on Jackson, between Sansome and Montgomery. John Cowell was merchandising on the corner of Sansome and Jackson; and the Commercial Hotel was kept by J. Ford & Co., on Jackson, between Montgomery and Sansome. Louis Cohn's store was in the same block. Myrie, Crosett & Co. were on Jackson, below Sansome. W. H. V. Cronise and Titus Cronise were auctioneers on the corner of Jackson and Montgomery. We would like one per cent. on all the money made by W. H. V. Cronise in San Francisco, or upon the amount he has given away in charity during the past twenty-four years. The Dalton House was on Jackson street, below Montgomery, and conducted by C. A. Smith. Dupuy, Foulkes & Co. were on the corner of Jackson and Battery; their store standing on piles, and accessible by a narrow sidewalk over the water of the bay. There were others on Jackson street whom we cannot recall, nor do we wish to compete with Kimball's Directory for 1850.

Until along into the summer of 1850, the sidewalks on Montgomery street ended a few steps south of California street, and the deep, slippery, shifting sand, checked the pedestrian's ardor very quickly after walking a block, more or less—generally less. When one had walked to Lütgen's Hotel, about half way between Pine and Bush streets, on the east side of Montgomery, he began to think that he would postpone his exercise for that day. Dr. Enscoe's house stood on the corner of Bush and Montgomery — southeast corner. Opposite was a long, rambling, three-story, pitched-roof wooden building, called the American Hotel, kept by a German. On the northwest corner of Bush and Montgomery was a grocery kept by a German. Our German citizens have, from the earliest of San Francisco's days, noted the importance of corners—the chances of a man halting at the corner; the probabilities of a man meeting some friend just turning the corner, and the great odds that they will halt and chat on the corner; the great likelihood of strangers stopping in to inquire for some one living in the vicinity. Corner property, of course, is a kind of "corner" on pedestrians.

On the southeast corner of Montgomery and Pine streets there used to stand one of those corrugated-iron buildings, many of which were imported from Europe, in pieces all numbered, and ready for erection. Berenhart, Jacoby & Co. were its occupants. On the southwest corner of the same streets was a little, unpainted wooden building, one and a half stories; a grocery, kept by a German, of course. This little store stood on the same corner until it was demolished to make way for the Russ House.

Small, dilapidated and insignificant as it was, we felt a little pang of regret when witnessing its demolition. The long, dry seasons of many summers had given it the look of half a century. The boisterous, tossing winds had thrown upon its little roof the dried seeds of vegetation, which the alternating rains woke into green life; and on shelves across the sills of the little windows, just beneath the venerable-looking eaves, were humble little flowers in improvised pots, once containing McMurray's oysters and Kensett's green corn.

The present site of the Lick House was in those days, and in fact, up to '58 or '59, a sand waste, unoccupied, save by the tents of some parties camping there, preparatory to going up-river to the mines; or, in later years, when it boasted the dignity of an enclosure for cattle on sale, a circus troupe, or industrial exhibition. The opposite side of the street was mostly a sand waste; the line of the street only marked by fragile structures, few and far between.

Kearny street was more populous and frequented, though its narrow sidewalks were fearfully and wonderfully made,—the work of many hands, and composed of a great variety of queer materials. In front of one man's property, the walk was made of barrel-staves, nailed upon stretchers; the next one adjoining had thin, springing boards, threatening at every step to let you through; then a mosaic, made of sides and ends of packing-cases, some portions covered with tin or zinc—the jagged, saw-like edges making business for the dealers in boots and shoes; now you trod upon the rusty tops of some old stoves, or heavy iron window-shutters, or an old ship's hatchway covering; then a dozen or two heads of kegs, set close together, imbedded in the mud of last year's rainy season; and so on, in great and curious variety.

In many places these odd patches of sidewalk ended with astonishing abruptness, as the unwary stranger, walking that way after dark, very suddenly discovered, as he plunged forward, jarring his entire frame, jerking off his hat into the mud or dust (as the season rendered propitious), biting his tongue, and altogether angering and discomposing himself, if he were not so unfortunate as to fall at full length, soiling and tearing his clothing or dislocating his limbs. The northern end of Kearny street, between Washington street and the Graham House (afterwards used as the City Hall), was the abode and resort of Mexicans, Peruvians, and Chilenos; while the southern part of the street was occupied by Germans and French, displaying Gast-haus and Café sign-boards, wine-merchants and bier-halles, Pharmacie-Francaise and Deutsche-Apotheke. The old Kearny street, with its narrow way; its slopy, uneven, ricketty, pitfall-sidewalks; its toppling, unsightly buildings and aggravating doorsteps, viciously projecting half way across the footpath; its ankle-deep sand of summer and knee-deep mud of winter, at the crossings;—that old Kearny street has passed away—thank Heaven, forever! What a contrast the corner of Post and Kearny presents. Where the dingy, old grocery once stood, with its stolid, phlegmatic proprietor, in soiled shirt-sleeves and unkempt locks, pipe in mouth, and hands in his pockets, obstructing his own doorway,—we now look upon the spacious and elegant White House— its grand show windows of clear plate-glass, displaying with artistic arrangement the costliest fabrics from the looms of India and Europe. Laces, too exquisite for man to describe or appreciate, but gazed upon by the gentler sex with the heightened color, parted lips, and sparkling eyes, betokening full recognition of their value. Everything in dry goods, from the soft, thick, warm, downy blanket, delighting the eye of poor, old, rheumatic women, to the floating folds of vaporous fabric, wonderfully ornamented for a bridal veil; and story upon story, piled with linens, silks and velvets, and shawls of every value. We are lifted, noiselessly, in a luxurious car, from floor to floor, where well-dressed, courteous, gentlemanly clerks, and our "old time" friends, George Huntsman and Raphael Weill, anticipate our slightest wish. And was it here that the old, dingy grocery and Assembly Hall stood? Surely, the late Horace M. Whitmore, who first projected this improvement, was no false prophet, when he said, "I'll alter Kearny street so that its oldest inhabitant will fail to recognize it!"

Lütgen's Hotel stands to-day in the same spot on Montgomery street, where it was originally built in 1849—just opposite where the Russ House now stands. It is a strong wooden building, of two stories, and a high, sloping roof. The second story originally projected in a kind of balcony over the sidewalk, its stout timbers having some little pretensions to carving; reminding one of quaint, old buildings in the cities and provincial towns of Europe. This building had a substantial, old-fashion appearance, greatly at variance with the pine-board shanties and wide-crannied structures usual at that time. Until quite recently this building presented its original front to the street. We miss the old, familiar object—its sturdy, honest timbers had stood so long, firm and unscathed by time, or change, or oft-repeated conflagration,—doing good service in these later years to set aright the puzzled visitor from the interior, who, once so familiar with the street, now seemed a stranger in a strange land, until the old landmark gave him his bearings, and sent him on his way, musing on reminiscences *tiempo pasado*.

Many of our well known German citizens boarded at Lütgen's in '49 and '50, and later still. Nicolas Luning and A. Von der Meden were there when we first knew them. It was quite remote from the city's bustle then. Especially did it seem so at night, so dark and still—no street lamps; no illuminated shopwindows—the deep sand muffling every footfall; a long, lonesome way to California street—plodding on in the soft, unstable sand—longer and more dreary than can be realized to-day by him who walks from Meyer's ivory-turning shop—that's where Lütgen's stood—to Wells, Fargo & Co's corner. Yet, the old citizen can remember the sigh of satisfaction with which he stepped upon the narrow strip of sidewalk in front of Howard & Green's iron store, south of California street, even if that sidewalk were but a narrow plank, laid for single file promenading.

CHAPTER VII.

The fire of May 4th, 1851, originated in the paint store of Mr. Oliver, on Clay street, Plaza, above Kearny, about eight o'clock on a Saturday evening, and its progress was so rapid, that people occupying houses a block away were unable to remove their goods. The roofs of buildings, seemingly too remote for danger, caught fire like powder, the flames creeping from street to street like a laid train, finding fresh combustible in the dry board walls, paper and cloth interiors; and the wind—sleeping at the fire's commencement—now roaring like a pyromaniac, tossed the blazing brands and glowing embers far away, igniting new fires upon distant roofs, till people thought incendiaries were consummating preconcerted deviltry, adding new horror to the dire confusion. The streets were crowded with loaded drays; the snorting teams, hurried by greedy drivers to some place of safety to unload, rush back and close with the highest bidder for another freight. Frantic men stood at their store doors, tossing their hands in the air, offering twenty! forty! fifty dollars a load, for the removal of valuable goods; but soon the streets became so blocked with teams and furniture and bales of goods, and hurrying, crowding men and mules, that the excited drivers, hoarse with shouting, in the vain effort to haul their goods, and win the rich harvest of fire-tariffs, were glad to unload and escape with teams and vehicles, some of them having only time to unhitch their animals, leaving their loaded drays to burn—losers in the battle, despite two or three loads at fire prices. Men stayed by their stores, hoping against hope, until the heat was unendurable, then ran for their lives, and many there were who lost the dreadful race. Ten or twelve bodies, charred beyond all recognition, were found in the streets after the fire subsided. Several men remained in the store of Taaffe & McCahill, corner of Sacramento and Montgomery, believing it to be fire-proof. When the heat became too intense, they tried to escape, but the swollen iron doors prevented. They fled to the cellar, seeking safety in a massive vault, where their remains were found. One of these unfortunate victims was Captain Vincent, the father of Mr. Vincent, of Vincent & Lewis, now of this city.

Mygatt & Bryant were the proprietors of the Washington Baths, corner of Washington street and Maiden Lane. The fire of May, '50, wiped out their establishment. They built it up again, painted and decorated it in good style, and were to open on the fourteenth of June; but, on that day, another fire came, saving them the trouble. Calvin Nutting had his iron works on Maiden Lane, between the bath rooms of Mygatt & Bryant and Jackson street. Mr. Nutting met the bath-house proprietors in the lane—or on the ground where the lane used to be—the day of the fire, and asked them if they were going to build again. They said, not unless they could build fire-proof, which, they supposed, was impossible. Mr. Nutting assured them that he could build them a fire-proof house; and before they parted a verbal contract was made.

The work was commenced in a few days, and satisfactorily finished; Mr. Nutting receiving his money in weekly or semi-monthly payments, as suited the convenience of Messrs. M. & B., until the contract was fully and faithfully complied with. We do not remember the cost of iron shutters and iron work for the fire-proof buildings in those times; but we know that it was very steep, and, when the fiery ordeal came, very few of the so-called fire-proof buildings stood the test.

We remember, as well as if it were but yesterday, being in front of Jo. Bidleman's fine, three-story brick, fire-proof store, on the east side of Montgomery street, between Washington and Jackson, when the fire of May 4th, 1851, reached it. Every one said, "Oh, the fire will stop there! It can't get through those walls and shutters!" But when the dreadful heat had turned its all-devouring breath upon the firm, thick walls, and bolted, massive shutters, the moments of suspense for the spectator were but few. He saw, along the iron window-shutter's edge, a line of thin, smoky fringe, like an angola edging for a lady's robe. For a moment it slowly curled about the window-casing; then, with a sudden puff, the delicately waving border quickly changed to a thick frame of wool-like smoke. The doubled sheets of bolted iron trembled and filled out like window-curtains shaking in a breeze, then burst their fastenings, belching long-tongued flames, that soon consumed the costly structure. We ran away from the fearful heat to the corner of Jackson street, and stopped to look upon the walls, melting like snow drifts, piled upon the edge of a long sleeping crater, suddenly aroused to angry violence. Our faith in "*fire-proof*" was shaken. Turning away, we saw the deep hollow on the northwest corner of Jackson and Montgomery—a weedy basin in dry weather, a murky pool in winter—filled with goods of all descriptions, rescued from the flames. We looked around, thinking how strange that all those goods should have been hurried there to save them from fire, and left wholly unprotected, no one watching them; the owners returned for more; gone for some refreshment, wearied to sleep, or what not? No one was there; all seemed deserted; and yet, half a block away, the shouts of frenzied men and bellowing roar of flames were unabated. Lying upon some boxes in the promiscuous pile, we saw the silver-plated frame and plate-glass of a jeweler's show case, with its velvet lining, and diamonds in their various styles of setting,—rings, brooches, pins, ear drops and bracelets, displayed in their caskets, as when spread for sale.

We thought the people mad—leaving those jewels there—and proposed taking them from their caskets, wrapping them in our handkerchiefs, and advertising them, after the fire. One thought we'd better leave them alone; another said: "Don't open the case! some one might be concealed among these piles of goods, watching them; and, taking us for thieves, shoot us!" We fell back at this, arguing the question.

One said that he was sure he knew the goods; they were Hayes & Lyndall's, in Clay street; and, knowing them to be good fellows, it was wrong in us to leave their goods to be stolen; to which another answered: "It isn't reasonable to suppose they are left unguarded." While thus conversing, we had slowly moved from the immediate neighborhood of the treasure, half-turned towards, and looking at it, when a gang of drunken, shouting vagabonds—just such as hung about the dens on the hillside at the heads of Montgomery and Kearny streets—came along Montgomery, from the burning buildings, and, sauntering into the hollow, saw the show-case and sprang upon it, tearing it open, snatching the contents, pushing and fighting for their booty, and yelling in drunken, thieving triumph.

The day after the fire of May 4th, 1851, two young men who had roomed together, and had lost by the conflagration all, save the clothes in which they stood, and a few dollars in their pockets, were hunting for a place in which to sleep. It was about noon, and they were very much fatigued and weary of going from one public house to another, finding them all full, crowded with men who had been sleeping in their stores and offices, as was customary in those days. Wandering on, they came to the St. Francis Hotel, on the corner of Dupont and Clay, and ascending the outside stair, walked along the balconies that reached around each story of the building. Finding one door ajar, they pushed it open carefully and looked in. The room seemed deserted and unfurnished, save a small stretcher for a single cot— just the wooden frame and canvas stretcher— no bedding. Stepping into the room, supposing it to be unoccupied, they were surprised to see a man standing just behind the door. He was a tall, powerfully built man, and stood with his head drooping upon his chest; his hands, or rather his wrists, crossed, as if he wished to keep his hands from touching anything. As the two intruders began to apologise for their unceremonious entrance, the man raised his head and waved his hands, with a gesture deprecating any apology, saying, in strangely muffled, indistinct speech, "Excuse me, but I do not know where I am, or how I came here." Just then—becoming accustomed to the dim light of the room, which so obscured everything on their entrance out of the bright sunlight—the friends saw that the man was dreadfully burned, his lips so swollen and distorted as almost to preclude intelligible utterance; his eyes closed, and the lids entirely indistinguishable; his quivering hands, which he held away from himself lest contact should increase their torture, so shockingly burned that the spectators sickened at sight of them. The beard was gone, and all the hair below the line of his hat-brim was completely gone. His head was uncovered; his scorched and battered hat lying in the middle of the floor, and all around and on the crown of his head were thick, light-red curls. There was something in the figure and action of the man—something even in his voice, muffled and disguised as it was, through his burned, shapeless lips—which seemed strangely familiar to the two men, as they listened intently, with great difficulty comprehending the statement of the sufferer. As he was telling them how he remained too long in his office, getting valuable papers together, in case the fire should reach the building and compel him to remove them to a place of safety; how he was unable to get out when the building took fire; and the iron doors, closed for safety, were so swollen by heat, that he could not effect his escape until aided by some people outside, attracted by his cries—he suddenly paused, and asked, "Don't you know me? I am Austin, your counselor!" It was Elbridge

Gerry Austin, the friend and legal adviser of the two men whom accident had led to the rescue. With increased interest and sympathy they hurried out, obtained a vehicle, tenderly placing him therein, and conveyed him to the house of Mr. C. W. Jones (of George N. Shaw & Co.), just south of Pine street, near Battery, where he was kindly nursed to recovery by the wife of his old friend and hospitable host. Ministering to the needs of one so much more unfortunate than themselves, quite banished all thoughts of their own troubles—newly impressing the *dos amigos* with a just appreciation of the value of health and unimpaired faculties; and walking back across the smoking ruins to that portion of the city undevastated, they found quarters with Bowman & Thacher, who, just burned out at the corner of Clay and Montgomery, had leased storeroom on board the storeship *Arkansas*, lying on the north side of Pacific wharf, between Sansome and Battery. Satisfied with the good work chance had placed in their hands, and weary with forty-eight hours of action, the two friends fully enjoyed their sleep in the comfortable old state-room provided for them.

Another incident of the same conflagration we recall. Two young fellows who came together to San Francisco, and were room-mates, losing all, save one little trunk-full of toilet indispensables, retreated before the devastating flames until they found themselves on the hillside, where Montgomery street led to Telegraph Hill, and here they sat down to watch the flames. Jaded out, and perfectly aware of the uselessness of fighting the devouring element, they concluded to climb the hill and seek some nook where they might sleep undisturbed. They soon reached a little valley or level spot, just beyond the first hill, about half-way to the summit, and saw a little cottage with sheltering veranda— extremely inviting to houseless vagrants. There was no light or evidence of life within. All seemed supernaturally quiet; the first faint gray of dawn was in the eastern sky; the elevation of the land toward the city hid the dense clouds of smoke, and the low, lurid flames, well nigh exhausted by their carnival. So strange seemed the stillness after the nerve-straining babel of excitement during the past seven or eight hours, that, actuated by a simultaneous impulse, they hurried to the little eminence and looked down upon the smoking ruins. The fire was low and darkly red, like a great bed of lava, and the black smoke rolled over the bay, as silent as a picture. Not an audible sound came to their ears; the shouting of men had ceased; the fire's exulting roar was hushed; both man and the scourging element seemed exhausted. Turning back, thoughtful and silent from the strange sight, they placed their trunk upon the veranda and laid down to rest. Just as they were sinking into unconsciousness, a woman's voice aroused them, inquiring why they were there. Hastily rising, they explained. The woman was much surprised, saying that just after herself and husband had retired, there came a messenger from Dewitt & Harrison's store, on Sansome, near Broadway, where her husband was the porter, requesting him to come down, as there was a big fire under way which might reach their building. The high wind, awakened by the fire, had blown the noise away from the remote and quiet locality, and she had gone to sleep all unconscious of the great calamity. With genuine hospitality and womanly sympathy, she invited them in, apologising for their scanty accommodations, and regretting that she had no bed to offer them, but refusing, despite all their entreaties, to allow them to sleep in the cold morning air, until she had prepared them some breakfast. By the time that daylight came, a hot breakfast with delicious coffee was set before them, filling them with refreshing comfort, and banishing all thoughts of sleep or weariness. With grateful hearts they expressed their many thanks, and departed. Often since has their gratitude been expressed, and the incident never will be forgotten.

CHAPTER VIII.

The Baltimore Boys always took a prominent part in the affairs of San Francisco, and on the right side of all momentous local issues.

Peter Stroebell was one of the good men of our early days—a man with a woman's heart and lion's frame, noble in stature and in nature, full of generous impulses and great integrity—as incapable of a mean action as of wearing the garments of a little man.

Mr. Stroebell went from San Francisco to Melbourne, Australia, on board the steamer *Monumental City*, of which he was agent and a large owner. The steamer was lost there, and Mr. Stroebell perished with her. The news of his death made sad the heart of every one who had known him.

George Hossefross was another Baltimorean; as true as steel, as open and honest as the sun, seeking with full hands the needy, and happiest when making others happy. He was one of the founders of the Monumental Engine Company, and was chief engineer of the San Francisco Fire Department.

James Hassan was a Baltimorean and a worthy confrére of his fellow citizens in California.

Hillard & Rider were Baltimoreans. John Rider died (we believe) in Nicaragua. B. F. Hillard is with the San Francisco Stock Exchange.

Ross Fish was, for many years, in San Francisco; but for the past ten years has been in the Treasury Department in Washington.

Wm. H. Hoburg was in business on Clay street in 1849–'50 with Bennett & Kirby, near Pioche, Bayerque & Co.'s store. Subsequently he was State Gauger. He is the same to-day as he was twenty-four years ago. Impulsive as a boy; utterly unable to be a hypocrite; everything for truth, but nothing for policy. Wet feet on Sherman's Island are, with him, far preferable to the dry shoes of some San Francisco Honorables.

Charley Warner possessed all the noble traits of his companions. His life was a bitter disappointment. Brought up to a mercantile life in a prominent South American house, with the promise of a partnership in the firm, after a term of years. The promise was a falsehood; and Warner, after serving faithfully for years, was displaced to give his well-earned position to a nephew of the man who had deceived him. From this wrong he never rallied; and although now beyond all earthly disappointment, still, his living friends to-day are touched with sadness at the recollection of his sorrows.

Dr. A. J. Bowie is from Baltimore. His skill as a surgeon is too well known for any mention in these pages. We could not describe his conversational powers, however great our desire. Madame de Stael, Talleyrand, Agassiz, Daniel Webster, Theodore Parker or Starr King, could have found enjoyment in listening to Dr. Bowie.

Julius C. McCeny is from Baltimore and a pioneer. He came to California when a lad, made money sufficient to study and graduate with honors at Harvard College, and returned to practice law in the Courts of California.

Winter & Latimer were Baltimoreans. A. B. McCreery was one of their employees in '49 and '50.

Dungan, Moore & Pendergast, on California street, were Baltimoreans.

James H. Wethered was from Baltimore; he was very successful, and had every prospect of wealth; but by some rascally maneuvering he was robbed of a fortune. We have heard him state the character and standing of the distinguished gentleman (with an "*Hon.*" prefixed to his name) who robbed him, and use every taunt to call him to a personal account; but the honorable gentleman always withdrew with celerity at Mr. Wethered's approach.

Wm. Divier, the former Superintendent of Streets, Beverly C. Saunders, Jo. Capprise, Tom. Hamilton, Robert Bennett, Tom. Lamb and John L. Durkee were from Baltimore; but John Whitehead was not, as many supposed, a native of the "Monumental City," but a North End Boston Boy.

There used to be in '49–'50 and on into '51, a man, who stood every morning on the corner of Long Wharf (now Commercial street) and Montgomery street, selling the "*Alta California.*" He always stood on the southeast corner, just at the curbstone, his broad-brimmed felt hat down over his eyes, hiding them and the expression of his face. He held the papers over his left arm, his left hand extended beyond the piled-up papers, just from the press. He stood like an automaton, never moving from his position, never raising his head, but exclaiming, at regular intervals, "Mornin' Pa–p–u–z! Mornin' Pa–p–u–z!" the accent on the last syllable of the second word. The fingers of the extended hand closed on each two-bit piece, as it was dropped into it, when the right hand came swinging slowly towards the coin, dropped upon it like some slow, awkwardly moving machinery, grappled it, and slowly swung it to the capacious pocket in the right side of his heavy pilot-cloth monkey-jacket, the action and movement reminding one of a derrick-crane lightering coals. We never heard any one ask the price of a paper; we never saw any hesitation on the part of seller or purchaser; everybody seemed to understand that it was "*dos reales.*" We have stood long and often, to see if the old fellow would utter something more than the stereotyped "M–o–r–n–i–n' P–a–p–u–z!" but he never did; nor did he ever sell any other paper than the "*Alta*," notwithstanding his cry of M–o–r–n–i–n' P–a–p–u–z!" The plural, doubtless referred to the number of "*Altas*," and he did sell a goodly number for many, many mornings, and realized a nice little sum in disseminating the news of the day and the well-written editorials of Frank Soulé, Durivage and the late lamented Gilbert and McDermott.

The *Alta California* office was on Washington street, just at the upper northwest corner of the Plaza, in 1850. Gilbert, Durivage and Kemble were editors. Frank Soulé and McDermott were subsequently on the editorial staff. Paul Morrell, of the Sacramento *Union*, was foreman of the *Alta* printing-office. One evening, we were walking up Washington street, when we met Mr. Morrell. "Turn about!" said he, "Come and see me win a diamond-cluster pin which is to be raffled in the Bella Union." "How many tickets have you," we inquired. "One! that is all that's required," he said. "Yes, if you happen to hold that particular one," we replied. "Here it is," said Don Pablo, holding up a ticket. We went in, and he did win it, and wears the same pin to-day.

Kemble was on the editorial staff of the *California Star*, afterwards continued under the name of the *Alta California*. He was a very elegant-looking young fellow in those days; and, when we in our unsophisticated youth first saw him *cavaliering* along Montgomery street, on his showy, black, high-stepping charger, with full, flowing mane and tail, saddle and bridle profusely decked with glittering, jingling silver ornaments, we thought surely this is some *hidalgo*. He sat so proudly in the saddle; his broad-brimmed *sombrero* worn with such a Castilian air; his rich waving hair, black, arching eyebrows, and long, fringing lashes; his blue coat and gold buttons, and long, bright, buckskin gauntlets, were a picture to look upon. We thought our informant was jesting when he said 'twas only an editor; he looked so like an Andalusian grandee. In after years, we became well acquainted with Kemble, and found him a real good fellow—fully equal to any "grandee" we ever knew.

In the *Polynesian* of June 27, 1846, we read: "The arrival of the *Brooklyn*, 136 days from New York, with 178 emigrants for California, has created no little interest in our town." In the same article we read: "Mr. Brannan has a press with him, and intends establishing a paper, to be called the *California Star*."

In the Mercantile Library rooms on Bush street, are bound volumes of the *California Star*, published by S. Brannan, Kemble editor. These volumes were presented to the library by Messrs. Barry & Patten.

"Tip" was no insignificant *attache* of the *Alta* office. Many men remember "Tip," a big terrier, black and brown—more brown than black. Every man and boy who knew the *Alta* knew "Tip." His office was no sinecure. Rats were in San Francisco by the million in those days, and if we could have a dollar, or even a dime, for every rat who received his *quietus* from "Tip," we should have far more capital than some of the bankers commenced with in early times. The rats of San Francisco and Sacramento in 1850, and up to the middle of the year 1853, were something wonderful. Should those pests swarm the stores, houses and streets to-day, as they did then, people would be frightened, and not without cause. The little, four-footed, rodent devils worked damage only second to the fires of that time. Warehousemen were put to their wits to circumvent them. Zinc and tins were nailed about the floors and lower boarding, like sheathing on a ship, and signs assuring "rat-proof storage" were plentiful and necessary. At dusk, the rats ventured boldly out upon the streets, racing and scampering incessantly; darting in every direction—squeaking and fighting with that vicious spitefulness natural to them. Pedestrians and new comers felt, as they walked among the countless swarm, a constant apprehension of treading upon the wicked little vermin; nor was the new comer alone so annoyed. We never could cure ourselves at times, of suddenly halting and lifting our hands quickly upward, when some big fellow sprang within an inch of us, or struck us full and heavy, as was not uncommon. Sometimes, a very venomous rat, when struck at by the promenader, would show fight and be killed, rather than retreat. A terrier dog, or a good cat, commanded a big price in those times. The captain, cabin-boy, cook, or sailor who chanced to bring with him one of those much-coveted creatures, found solid consolation in separating from his faithful companion of the voyage.

Every dog or cat of them, however, became poisoned and off duty, on the sick-list very soon, the result of their incessant labors. As time went on, and brought more dogs and cats, the rat *commune* was thinned out, defeated and reduced to the ordinary number; so that the citizen of to-day cannot, like the early resident, distinguish the rat of Valparaiso, the rat of Canton or Singapore, the long, white, pink-eyed rice-rat of Batavia, the New York, Boston or Liverpool wharf-rat, nor yet the kangaroo rat from Australia—so well known and readily recognized in the days when they held high carnival in our streets, warehouses and dwellings.

CHAPTER IX.

Those who had eaten at the French restaurants, the LaFayette, the Jackson and the Franklin, until they were tired of the same flavors and odors, however changed and disguised by the artistic *chef;* or if not satiated by the complications and mysteries of the *cuisine*, if it chanced that finances were rather low, and ways and means were to be considered, and four bits instead of a dollar and a half must suffice for breakfast—one could get it for that sum, and very well cooked too, at the New York Bakery, on the same spot where it now stands, on the east side of Kearny street, between Clay and Commercial—though there was no Commercial street west of Montgomery street then. To be sure, the breakfast was not elaborate—a cup of coffee, two hot biscuit and a plate of baked beans—but they were very good; and though we went there first from necessity, we often went afterwards when we had plenty of the *collateral*, because the meals were so very good, so relishing, and such an agreeable diversion from richer, costlier and less digestible food. The Irving House, when it was opened, on the spot where Montgomery Block now stands, was a pleasant change to crowds of men without homes and family comforts; men who, as most all did in those days, slept in their offices or stores, taking their meals anywhere and everywhere, at French, Italian, Spanish, German or Chinese restaurants. So, when the Irving House was opened by Du Martrey & Mason, in the New York style, neat, clean, with quiet attendants and good cooking, with the welcome and familiar buckwheats and golden syrup, the San Franciscan began to feel as he skimmed the "*Alta*" or "*Herald*," while waiting for breakfast, as if the city of his adoption were becoming quite Americanized.

On the west side of Kearny, between Clay and Sacramento, was a little restaurant kept by Madame Rosalie, a vivacious little French woman, with the most piquant manner and conversation, and bewitching toilette. Her *chef* was an artist, and her little *salle a manger* was cosy and comfortable, the table linen and the equipage nice and clean, and her patronage the better class of citizens. We remember going in one morning to breakfast, and as we stopped a moment at the counter, to wish the fair hostess "Good morning!" a gentleman was asking if he could have some fresh eggs for breakfast. "How would Monsieur like zem?" inquired the polite little woman. "Boiled, if you please!" said he. "Oh!" said the Madame, her face assuming, quick as thought, the expression of one who had lost everything worth retaining on earth, her shoulders raising in the most expressive of shrugs, her little, speaking hands outstretched with upturned palms, and her whole manner the perfection of pantomimic apology, "Oh, pardon, Monsieur! very good for ze *omelette*, but not for ze *bouillie!*"

Raphael's restaurant was on Pike street, between Clay and Washington; a dingy, little yellow *casa*, externally, and dingier, smaller still, within. The bill of fare could be readily ascertained by a sensitive nasal organ, on entering the *salle a manger* which was separated from the kitchen by a dingy, tattered curtain, of unknown material, which offered no impediment to sound or odor from the *chef's* domain, nor softened in the least the high key of Raphael's loud vociferation, profuse in the profane *morceaux* of many nations, which he glibly hurled at French, Italian, Spanish, Portugese and English cooks and waiters. His vocalization had a running accompaniment of clashing fire-irons, rattling crockery and cooking utensils.

Breakfast in the main saloon, a room about fifteen by twenty feet, was one dollar without the extras, such as eggs, claret, etc. In the exclusive apartment, a little, hot, smoky coop, closer to the kitchen fire, and raised by a few steps from the common room, from which it was separated by a curtain, breakfast was half a dollar extra. Many of Raphael's patrons had known him in the Parker House, in Boston, and knowing his accomplishments as a *chef*, welcomed him to San Francisco, and are still loyal to him, wherever he wears the white cap.

After the guests became too numerous for the little place on *la rue de Pike*, Raphael came down to Sacramento street, on the north side, just above Montgomery, No. 51, where the business flourished, and his voice raised a semitone, and his loquacity increased. Of course he didn't stay here long. No one could remain in undisturbed prosperity in those days; it would have been too much good fortune. The fire soon swept everything away. Subsequently, this distinguished *chef* took the restaurant of the Tehama House, and to tell of all the places where he has since tickled the gastronome, would fill by far too many pages of this volume.

Jim D——, who came to San Francisco in 1847,—a happy, reckless, generous boy, ever ready for a spree, or real hard work to aid a friend; liberal to a fault; the best man *for* you, and the worst you could have *against* you,—was up from his ranch of many leagues, once upon a time, on a little *pasear* in San Francisco, when late one night he found himself sitting on a doorstep on the Washington street side of the Plaza. We have said he found himself sitting there—we should have said police-officer E—— found him sitting there, for Jim was *lost*—in meditation. Officer E—— came along, stopped a moment, and touched Jim upon the shoulder, but receiving no response, shook him gently. "What is it?" inquired Jim, without troubling himself to raise his head. "You must move on," said E——. "Oh, no, you're mistaken!" said Jim. "I'm very comfortable here; you had better move on yourself!" "Come, no nonsense," said E——, "you musn't sit here." "Well, I'll bet you *cinco pesos* that I do sit here just as long as I want to!" "Ah, indeed!" said the officer, "I see that I shall have to take you in." At this stage of the proceedings, Jim, for the first time condescended to raise his head. "Hallo!" he exclaimed in a surprised tone, "Isn't this E——?" "Yes, sir," answered

the guardian of the night "I'm Officer E——."
"Well, now, listen to me!" said Jim, putting his head a little forward and inclining it to one side, closing his twinkling black eyes, and pursing up his mouth in his own peculiar manner— "Listen! If you don't move on yourself and let me alone, I'll hiss your wife the first time I see her on the stage!" We must explain that Mrs. E——, was a member of the dramatic company then performing in the city—a charming actress, and most exemplary woman; and Officer E—— being a good husband and sensible man, *moved on*. It is unnecessary to say to anybody who knew Jim D—— that he never would have carried out so ungallant a threat; but his sense of humor and ready invention at *ruse de guerre*, would not allow him to lose the opportunity.

Apropos of humor and invention, we recall a very good thing of Ned B——, whose erratic doings and sayings were as familiar as amusing to all the old citizens. If Ned made ten dollars by writing ten lines of notarial manuscript, or ten thousand by some speculation, 'twas all the same. His object was to get rid of the money at once, in the quickest possible way— a dinner at the La Fayette or the Jackson House, a conflict with the striped king of the jungle, or a costly gift to some fair acquaintance. We remember that on the occasion of some wedding, reception, ball, or festivity of some kind, a young lady had said in Ned's hearing that she intended to wear a japonica in her hair, if her brother succeeded in finding one. Now, japonicas, or any other cultivated flowers, were rather costly in those days; a little bunch of violets, or a tiny bouquet, such as might be purchased to-day for two bits, was worth from two dollars and a half to ten dollars, as circumstances commanded. But this was nothing to be considered by Ned B——, who at once proceeded to the nearest florist's, where one solitary japonica was the cynosure of eyes. Several flower-hunters were eager to negotiate, but were appalled at the terms. "Have you any japonicas?" said Ned, bustling in. "There's the last one, sir," said the florist, with all the cool *sang froid* of one, master of the situation. "How much is it?" inquired Ned. "Fifty dollars!" said the modest disciple of Flora. "I'll take it," said B——, tossing down an auriferous octagonal, and calmly walking away to win one smile.

Some years later, when japonicas were more plentiful, but when, alas! "the root of all evil" had become inconveniently scarce, and expedients were absolutely necessary, Ned had a notarial commission, and his office was on Montgomery, near Merchant street. One morning a notice appeared in the daily papers, requesting the creditors of Saml. W—— and Frank T——, formerly residents of San Francisco, but at that time living in the city of New York, to present their claims against the above named gentlemen on or before the date mentioned in the advertisement. Early the next morning, the office of Mr. B—— seemed to be doing an unusual business. Many people were awaiting the advent of the notary who was collecting the claims against Messrs. S. W. and F. T. These kind people, in every trade and profession, old and young of both sexes, who had believed in the probity of S. W. and F. T., presented their respective accounts, which were carefully entered upon a formidable looking book, and each claimant requested to swear to his claim and pay the notarial fee of one dollar, which they cheerfully did, leaving the office and their claims, but taking with them new hopes. It was said at that time that six hundred and twenty-nine claims were left in the hands of the enterprising notary, for which privilege each individual paid the regular fee of one dollar.

It was also stated, but with what foundation we cannot say, that the claims averaged $200 each, making an aggregate of $125,800. From our personal knowledge of these "former residents," we conjecture that many confiding acquaintances either failed to read the notary's advertisement, or declined to present their "little bills." However, Ned B—— sported new and jaunty attire, and a rose-bud in his button-hole immediately subsequent to the filing of the claims at one dollar each.

CHAPTER X.

Leidesdorff street, as we have previously said, was originally a little levee, built along the beach, from a point near Sacramento street to Clay street, and a great convenience in those days it was, to come up in your boat alongside this levee, and step directly ashore, and pass up your baggage, without the necessity of wading and hauling your shallop up the beach.

On Clay street wharf, at the end of Leidesdorff, were the zinc-front stores occupied by Ferdinand Vassault, Simmons, Hutchinson & Co., J. J. Chaviteau, Selim and Edward Franklin, and the office of "up-river" steamboats.

We remember being in the office of the steamer "*McKim*," one afternoon in June, 1850, on some business with E. W. Bourne, purser of the "*McK.*" when a very stately individual, dressed in a very nice, new suit of navy blue, a glazed cap with brass buttons, a voluminous white collar, *a la Byron*, walked in. The dignified stateliness of his step, the manner of crossing his hands over his folded, but unbuttoned coat, his short neck, heavy features and long, dark hair, combed smoothly behind his ears, attracted our attention. Two or three bystanders touched their hats and saluted him as "*Capitan!*" as he walked on to an old-fashioned counting-house desk, at which stood an auburn-haired man, busy at his ledger. Some conversation ensued, which was not pleasing to the industrious clerk, who exploded with wrath. "Who the d——l cares whether you like it or not?" said he. "You can go to—" (here he named an exceedingly sultry climate) "if you don't like it!" Here the "Captain" drew himself up with impressive dignity, and attempted to speak, but the auburn-haired man rattled on: "Who the d——l do you expect to scare? You are nothing but a Mississippi steamboat clerk! You haven't been Captain long enough to know how to treat people, and you'd better go about your business and try to learn it." Completely vanquished, the "Captain" walked out in a manner strikingly different from that of his entrance; he of the auburn hair continuing a volley of complimentary shots, which gradually subsided as the defeated disappeared.

"Who is he?" inquired we of E. W. B., indicating by a nod of our head toward the departed. "That's Captain Charley B——, of the '*McKim*.'" "Who is he?" nodding toward the still growling man at the desk. "That is Tom. B——, the clerk!" "He will get his walking ticket, won't he?" "Not much!" said our friend, laughing loudly. "The boot is on the other leg—this is California!"

We walked away, musing upon the potentiality of circumstances.

The Pacific Mail Steamship Company had their office in Wm. D. M. Howard's building on Long Wharf, southeast corner of Leidesdorff, until the fire of June 14th, 1850, when they built at the corner of Sacramento and Leidesdorff, where they remained until the completion of their new wharf and offices, almost or quite twenty years.

Dall & Austin were on the southwest corner of Sacramento and Leidesdorff until the fourteenth of June fire, when they built a pier at the junction of Sansome and Sacramento streets.

Gay & Lovering were on the south side of Sacramento street, on the corner of a little alley which led through to California street, navigable, excepting at excessively high tides.

Robert Wells & Co. were commission merchants on Howison's Pier.

Locke & Morrison were commission merchants at the foot of Sacramento street. Wilmot Martin was with L. & M. in those days.

Hussey, Bond & Hale were on Howison's Pier at a later day.

B. Triest's store was on Sacramento, between Sansome & Battery—Howison's Pier.

Benjamin H. Freeman, stair builder, was on the corner of Sacramento and Montgomery, twenty-two years ago; his office to-day is in the Board of Fire Commissioner's rooms, of which Board he is a worthy and respected member.

Nathaniel Gray, now on the corner of Sacramento and Webb, was, in the "spring of '50," on the corner of Sacramento and Dupont. His advertisement in the "*Alta California*" of that date, informed the public that he sold metallic burial cases, exchange on New York, purchased gold dust, and gave particular attention to the undertaking business. By easy analogy, we next come to those whose profession it is to execute the testamentary wishes of the men whose mortal remains have been consigned to the dust from whence they came.

Halleck, Peachy & Billings were occupying offices on Sacramento street, between Montgomery and Kearny. Subsequently they removed to chambers in their own building—

Montgomery Block, on the southeast corner of Washington and Montgomery. Gen. Halleck's history is world-wide, and Messrs. Peachy & Billings are both too well known to require any comment in these pages.

Lambert & Co. (F. F. Low was the Co.) had their store on Sacramento, between Kearny and Montgomery streets.

Fitzgerald, Bausch, Brewster & Co. were on the same street, near Lambert & Co.

Everett & Co. (Theo. Shillaber) were on Howison's Pier.

Joseph S. Spinney's shipping office was on the wharf, at the foot of Sacramento street.

Mohler, Caduc & Co. had an office on Howison's Pier—Phil. Caduc built the pier. M. & C. were in the ship-storage business. They had the brigs *Piedmont* and *Casilda* off the end of the pier. Ship-storage was profitable for those in the business, and very safe and fortunate for the owners of the goods, when one of the sweeping conflagrations came. It was also convenient for lightering goods to the up-river steamers, saving wharfage and drayage. Our amiable friend Caduc appears to-day just as he did twenty-three years ago. We do not see any difference in his bright eye, black hair and beard, or in his erect figure and quick step.

He has taken life very coolly for many years, supplying our ardent and impetuous fellow-citizens with ice. Mohler, his former partner, we have not heard of for many years.

Howison's Pier commenced at the corner of Leidesdorff and Sacramento streets, on the south side of Sacramento street, as if it were a continuation of the south sidewalk, a narrow, little strip, just wide enough for a hand-car tramway, and room each side for one person to walk. When you came to Sansome street (or the line of it, for there was no street then) there was a little pier, built out from Howison's Pier, running north, and on the east line of Sansome street. This pier or wharf was just long enough to accommodate the store of Dall & Austin.

The store-ship *Thomas Bennett* was on the south side of Howison's Pier, at the corner of Sansome street, and was headquarters for the Baltimore boys, Messrs. Stroebell, Ayer, Ross Fish, Hoburg, Hillard, Ryder, Warner, Bennett, McCeny, Hossefross, Hassam, the Gough brothers, John L. Durkee, Billy Buckler and many others.

The corners of Sansome, Battery and Sacramento streets were originally built of piles— little piers, just large enough to accommodate the stores and premises forming the junction of the streets. At high tide goods could be lightered from the shipping to the stores, and from the stores to the Sacramento and Stockton steamers. After a while, a narrow row of piles was driven from Sacramento street (Howison's pier) to Commercial and on to Clay street, and then extended to Washington, on to Jackson and to Pacific. Upon the head of these piles was nailed a narrow plank walk, about four feet wide, without rail or protection of any kind whatever. Along this narrow way pedestrians passed and repassed in the dark, foggy nights, singing and rollicking, as unconcernedly as if their path was broad Market street, instead of an unprotected four foot wide plank walk, with drowning depth of water awaiting the unwary traveler who might miss his footsteps.

Near Jackson street, a coffee-house was built and kept by W. Meyer, where the traders of Pacific, Jackson and Clay street wharves, and the masters of ships in that vicinity, could get the best coffee in town, without the inconvenience of walking all the way to Portsmouth Square.

When the plank-road was built to the Mission Dolores, the tollgate was placed on Third street, west side, about the southern line of Stevenson street. In those days, when you had turned the corner of Third street to Mission street, going west, you were pretty well out of town. Opposite the Howard cottages, where the Howard Presbyterian Church now stands, was quite a lagoon, never wholly dry in summer, and in the rainy season, deep enough to drown anybody. When you had gone along the plankroad as far as Sixth street, you came to a bridge, across a marsh. Just before reaching this bridge, on the right hand side of the road, was the entrance to the Yerba Buena Cemetery. On the left of the road, nearly opposite the cemetery gate, was the residence of C. V. Gillespie, a pleasant, home-like residence, grateful to eyes becoming familiarized with board shanties, tents, and one-story, oblong, flat-roofed dwellings, shooting forth long, blackened, unstable stovepipes. This pretty dwelling, with its high enclosure and quiet seclusion, its climbing vines, its bright window-panes and neat curtains, its substantial sheltering roof and chimneys, standing upon the eminence just before you began to descend to the bridge, was so unlike our homes in the California of those days, and so like the old homes on the Atlantic shore, that we often used to think it was more affectingly eloquent to the giddy, prosperous, thoughtless young men who galloped past, to and from the Mission and the *milk punch*, than the most solemn sermons preached at stated hours in all the churches.

When past the bridge, and going up the rise the other side, we saw a little house, not much larger than a full-sized Saratoga trunk, from the roof of which bravely pointed a flagstaff, with the stars and stripes, and on the door of which was the word "Pipesville." This was the country-seat and poet's corner of the well known "Jeems Pipes," Stephen C. Massett, whose songs and music are far better than thousands over which the world makes more noise and gives far greater credit; whose recitations, imitations and essays, both humorous and pathetic, are so genuinely good, that we are puzzled by the reflection—why is he not rich? and recall the old adage, "A prophet has no honor in his own country."

Evrard & Robinson were the proprietors of the Dramatic Museum, on California street, between Montgomery and Kearny, in 1850.

Dr. Robinson, in 1851, opened the American Theatre, on the corner of Sansome and Halleck streets, and did a great business there. Biscaccianti, under the management of George Loder, made her *debut* before a California audience in this theatre. Kate Hayes, Emily Coad, Miss Sophie Edwin, Miss Sue Robinson (daughter of the manager), Emily Thorne, Julia Pelby, and a score of lesser celebrities, filled engagements there.

One evening, when some unusual attraction was on the boards, and the house was uncomfortably crowded and exceedingly hot, an American Sovereign, evidently from "Pike," occupying a seat in the front of the dress-circle, finding the atmosphere too sultry, arose upon his feet, and deliberately pulled off his coat, laid it upon the seat, and sat down in the comfort of shirt-sleeves. This proceeding was observed by only a few in his vicinity, as the attention of the audience was given to the play, which just at that moment was quite interesting; but the "gods," who act as mentors for the dress-circle just as severely as for the actors—always watchful for, and delighted with any slip-up in either place—detected this breach of etiquette before the offender had seated himself, and there arose from the sky-critics such a yell of derision that the words upon the stage were drowned. The actors ceased for a moment, entirely unconscious of the cause, supposing the tumult would subside; but, as the bumpkin culprit had no more idea than the greater part of the audience what the clamor meant, he sat, gaping at the gallery, wondering why the show didn't go on. All this time the actors stood in their places, while the babel swelled to something appalling, when some good-natured person touched the unconventional party upon the shoulder and explained the situation. The awful din ceased for an instant, as the *hydra* watched the dialogue. "Shirt-sleeves" seemed refractory—a terrific roar from the *hydra*— "Shirt-sleeves" quailed at the aspect, and the angry words of the impatient auditors in his immediate vicinity; started up with an air of coerced innocence, resumed his *toga virillis*, and his seat. The yell of triumph that arose from the "gods" in their joyful sense of victory, was beyond the description of tongue or pen. The play proceeded, and the dignity of San Francisco dress-circle etiquette was established.

CHAPTER XI.

The most wonderful case of mistaken identity, is that of Berdue, who was arrested and charged with the murderous assault upon Mr. Jansen, of Jansen, Bond & Co., and the robbery of their store on Montgomery street.

The general outline of this curious story is familiar to all old San Franciscans, and was published in the "Annals of San Francisco;" but the remarkable particulars, the facts of the case, are stranger than fiction—would in a romance be deemed overwrought. Thomas Berdue was arrested for the crimes above-mentioned, taken to the bedside of Mr. Jansen, who was supposed to be *in articulo mortis*, and recognized by him as the man who assaulted him. Another man was taken with Berdue to Mr. Jansen's bedside, but he pointed out Berdue at once as the criminal.

He was remanded to the jail, then in the Graham House, on the corner of Kearny, and was there tried for the crime, by the exasperated citizens, who no longer trusted the authorities; but the jury failed to agree. Then the citizens assembled to hang him, but were restrained by the military until calmer counsel prevailed. Meantime, Berdue had been recognized as the murderer and robber of Sheriff Moore, of Auburn, California, was taken there, tried, convicted and sentenced to death.

There was not the slightest room for doubt in the matter. Men who had known him in Australia, and men who had worked with him in the mines of California, swore positively that Berdue was not Berdue, but Stuart. They were not likely to be mistaken; the prisoner was a peculiar looking man, tall, inclined to stoop, his beard remarkably black, long and pointed, but his hair was a rich brown, fine and wavy, reaching below his collar. He had lost a joint from one of his fingers; had a little slit in one of his ears, and a scar over the left eyebrow. His eye was black, glittering and restless; his nose, aquiline; and he had a defiant way of raising his head and looking around him. In his gait there was a marked peculiarity, a long, measured step or stride, like one pacing the measurement of ground. The witnesses were not likely to be deceived, with all these peculiar marks of identity. Therefore, he was condemned to hang, and a very short time allowed him for preparation. While awaiting his sentence, there lay in the harbor of San Francisco an English merchant ship, which had brought a cargo to this port, and was about to sail for home. The Captain's wife was on board with him. One night, after they had turned in, they heard a sound like some one on deck. After listening a moment, without hearing anything more, they ceased to give it farther attention; but presently, hearing an unusual movement in the cabin, the Captain stepped out to ascertain the cause, when he was felled by a slung-shot, the same weapon used upon Mr. Jansen. The brave wife was grappling with the would-be murderer, before he could turn from his victim to robbery. This was an unexpected dilemma for the ruffian. He tried choking and "slung-shotting" her, but she clung to his hands with a tenacity that defeated him, and screamed with such a power in her desperation, that the alarm was quickly given, assistance promptly came, and the cowardly villain was soon in the hands of the Vigilance Committee on Battery street.

This was the real Stuart! the murderer of Sheriff Moore and the robber of Jansen. When he was brought to daylight, on the morning after his arrest, the people could scarcely realize that he was not the man already tried and condemned to death. When Berdue, who was innocent of all for which he stood accused, was placed beside the Australian convict and murderer, the resemblance was something more than wonderful; it was awful, under the circumstances!

Not only in stature, complexion, similarity of hair—soft, long, brown and waving over the shoulders—and long, black, pointed beards; but each had lost the joint from the same finger of the same hand; each had the little slit in the left ear; the same shaped scar over the left eyebrow; and when they stepped, there was the same peculiarity of gait. The physiognomist could see the aquiline nose, the very black eye, and habit of lifting the head to look around; but in Berdue's eye, the disciple of Lavater could not see the cold, wicked, cruel glitter noticeable in Stuart's eye, nor the devilish expression of his mouth and nostril. When Stuart was ordered to be brought out for sentence, the guard led him forward from the cell in the corner of the committee room to the Judge's seat. Stuart was taller than the guard on either side, and his arms were pinioned behind him. His black, piercing eyes glanced on every side, as he was led through the throng of men to the open space in front of the judgment seat. The guard halted with their prisoner directly before it. He fastened his gaze upon the Judge's calm, solemn face, with an intensity that was painful. Breathless silence prevailed for a moment. The Judge's voice pronounced the murderer's name, and proceeded with the usual form, reciting his crime and sentencing him to be taken from thence in two hours' time, and hung by the neck until dead, and exhorting him to make his peace with God, through the priests who were in attendance.

When the Judge's words broke the silence which fell upon the multitude, as the murderer paused to hear his doom, Stuart started, lifted his head defiantly, and stood like a statue until the sentence was spoken.

His burning eye was never for an instant diverted from the Judge's face, yet, by an indescribable flash, it seemed continually taking in everything around him, as if his sight and his attention were divided; fascinated by one object, from which he could not avert his gaze or thought; while watchful and intensely conscious of every movement and sound around him, like a ferocious beast of prey, surprised and angry at its capture, maddened with its fetters, keenly alert with the hope of escape and the desire to destroy its captors, but never a thought of sorrow or repentance.

At the close of the sentence, when the guard turned the prisoner back to the corner of the room, where the priests stood awaiting him, he strode forward with the peculiar step, characteristic of, and so nearly fatal to his double; but his features could not assume indifference. He seemed to be argus-eyed; to note the slightest movement near him, and to recoil from it with that indescribable mingling of fear, entreaty and defiance seen in the eyes of men awaiting the terrible details of execution. Within the appointed time, declining, scornfully, spiritual consolation, he was led down the stairs from the Vigilance Committee Rooms to the street, and escorted by hundreds of the members, each carrying a loaded revolver in his right hand, to a little pier on Market street, east of Battery, where the gallows had been improvised upon a derrick used for loading lighters.

The rope was placed around his neck, after some one had removed his hat for that purpose. Then, he who had removed the hat, a broad-brimmed, low crown, black felt hat, placed it upon his head so as to cover his features, and pressed the prisoner's hand, saying, "Be firm, and 'twill soon be over!" At a signal, the tall, silent figure was suddenly pulled against the outstretched arm of the derrick by hundreds of hands, grasping the long rope that led from the gallows to the rear rank of the band, that marched to justice one of the vilest outlaws who ever came from the penal colonies of Great Britain to the shores of California.

CHAPTER XII.

"Poverty makes strange bed-fellows." So did California in early days. Neither gold-dust, not yet silver dollars, would always avail in getting a room to one's self.. A little of the experience of those early days took the fastidiousness out of most men. Still, some never could, though half-dead with fatigue, obtain dreamless, refreshing sleep in blankets, the dread of contact with which made him lie down for the night in clothing worn all day, thus precluding the refreshment and freedom which disrobing gives the wearied body. Nor could he, predisposed to insomnia, sink to oblivion comfortably, after catching the glittering, furtive glare from the eyes of a silent, outstretched figure in the bunk above or below the one to be occupied by himself, under the pillow of which he had so quietly (thinking himself all unobserved) just then slid the little chamois-skin sack containing his entire "credentials."

Where the Cosmopolitan Hotel now stands,

there was in 1849, and into 1850, a sand-hill, nearly, if not quite as high as the spacious structure now forming the southwest corner of Bush and Sansome—a lonely, desolate looking spot even in daylight, and at night, a place to be avoided. In the middle of this sand-hill was a hollow, hidden from the sight of passers-by, either upon Montgomery street or the winding path from Macondray & Co's store (on the corner of Pine and Sansome), past Cy. Jones' little cottage, and skirting the lumber-yard of R. S. Dorr, or the path across the deep, toilsome sand-waste, afterwards occupied by the Oriental Hotel, and now by the warehouse and offices of L. & M. Sachs. In the little hollow of this sand-hill were tents and board shanties, and occasionally the deck-house or old galley of some ship, the occupant of which suddenly appearing in the low doorway, or showing a villainous-looking head, with tangled elf-locks and shaggy beard, at the little square port-hole window, like a bandit-portrait by Salvator Rosa, in a very scant frame—an apparition not in the least calculated to inspire confidence in the minds of those who, in broad daylight, had wandered there. On the contrary, an immediate desire seized one to regain the more frequented pathways skirting the lonely sand-hill's base. Runaway sailors, escaped convicts, burglars and desperados of every nation, skulked here by day, and prowled forth by night, to those acts of crime and violence which called into existence the Vigilance Committee of 1851. The path before mentioned, skirting the sand-hill rising from the corner of Bush and Battery, extended to where First street now joins Market street. There were buildings on both sides of First street. The tide came up under the workshops on the east side of the street. It was here that James and Peter Donahue commenced laying the foundation of the fortune which has ever since so generously aided all enterprise and charity, and every scheme for the advancement of public good, aside from private deeds of kindness, and "more good by stealth" than can be here recorded.

On the west side of this street were a few stores, lodging-houses, restaurants, and a butcher's shop. At the "Isthmus," kept by Mr. H——, Morpheus could be wooed for one dollar *cada noche*, and won—if the fleas were propitious. The sleeping conveniences were not quite Sardanapalian, being open bunks, in tiers three deep, a row on each side of the apartment, and one row reaching along the entire centre of the floor. Dingy gray blankets, and dingier pillows, *sans sachets*, were the accessories. Matutinal ablution was ignored by the worthy landlord. Still, this resting place was often chosen, because it was not quite convenient to pay three dollars *cada noche* for clean sheets and snowy pillow-cases at the St. Francis.

There was a boy (a native of Australia) who sometimes gave an exhibition of the manner in which the *boomerang* is thrown. He became known as an adept in casting the mysterious missile of Van Dieman's Land, and often he would be hired by people curious to see the *modus operandi*, and, as he passed along the streets to some large, open space, convenient for the feat, his audience would increase until the number afforded a very nice little contribution, when, subsequent to the performance, the hat was passed around. It was in the sand-hill where the Rassette House was afterwards built, and where the Cosmopolitan Hotel now stands, that the boomerang was thrown. The boy used to swing his body around to the right, sweeping the piece of thin, curved wood, like a scimetar, back as far as he could reach, then, quick as a flash, throwing it with all his force high up in the air before him.

It seemed to the spectator as if it went three hundred feet before it suddenly paused, trembled for an instant, and quickly slid back again, down the same path upon which it ascended, as if gliding along an invisible wire, until it fell upon the sand, a little distance to the rear of him who cast the queer projectile. There was an ale house called the "Boomerang," kept by Langley & Griffiths, on Kearny street, west side, just beyond Palmer, Cook & Co.'s Bank; a real English place, "with jolly good ale and old," with Cheshire and Stilton cheese, and, on stated days, a roasted sirloin, the sight, odor and taste of which excited in the breast of native Americans great respect for British meats and British cooking. The proprietors were good men, and much respected by the citizens. Newspaper men, literary men, actors, musicians and others who liked quiet and comfort, used to resort there to quaff the brown October, enjoy a good cigar, and look over the "London Times," the "Illustrated London News," "Punch," "Bell's Life" and "The Hue and Cry." "Jeems Pipes of Pipesville" was often here, and Jeems is, or ought to be, a judge of good ale.

The "Boomerang" has gone forever, like very many of its *habitues.* Its courteous hosts are—we know not where! New and pretentious buildings front upon the old site. Nothing remains save its memory, which is pleasant. *Requiescat in pace!*

We believe that Mr. Langley, of the firm of Langley & Co., druggists in this city, is a brother to mine host of the old "Boomerang."

Charley Elleard, as early as June, 1850, kept a bar and oyster room on Clay street, on the north side, about midway between Kearny and Montgomery. It was a very neat, stylish place. Oyster stews (canned oysters) were one dollar and fifty cents per plate, and considered very reasonable. Fresh oysters were unknown then; subsequently they were brought from Shoalwater Bay, by Captain Russell, and first sold by Toney Oakes, on Kearny street, north of Washington.

Charley Elleard was a constable in 1850, and in the execution of his official duties, rode a black pony, with white feet, a sagacious equine, the pet of everybody about Clay street and the neighborhood of the Plaza and adjacent Kearny street. His saddle and bridle were Mexican, gorgeously caparisoned with jingling silver, polished with care and glittering in the sun. He had learned the luxury of polished understanding; and if anybody would place a two bit piece in his mouth, straightway he would march to the bootblack stand on the southwest corner of Kearny and the Plaza, drop the money into the hand of the operator, put one hoof upon the boot-rest, quietly note its polishing, and when finished, raise the other, gravely wait its manipulation, then walk directly back to his master's office. His ponyship seemed to derive especial enjoyment from this maneuver; whether from the polish on his hoofs, or the prevalent custom of trying to see how much money he could spend, we do not know, but as two bit pieces were plenty, and the pony was always ready, he might often be seen as we have related.

Three years ago, Mr. Elleard, who was revisiting San Francisco, told us that the old pony was still living in his paddock in St. Louis, stone blind, and just able to walk across the ground, whinnying feebly, and rubbing his nose against his master's hand whenever he came to look upon his faithful old servant and companion.

Everybody in San Francisco knew the signal for a side-wheel steamer; and about the time one was expected with the mails, men used to come to their store doors and look up at the signal-house on Telegraph Hill, right in the line of Montgomery street. The signal for the side-wheel steamer, was like two outstretched, uplifted arms—two long, black boards, one on each side of the long, black signal pole.

Everybody knew this signal, and knew that

the P. M. S. S. Co's steamers were all side-wheelers, and citizens were so delighted to see the signal of "tidings from home," that it was an understood thing for men to suspend all business, and take a drink, in the pleasurable excitement of anticipation. A crowd at once besieged Adams & Co's office, impatiently waiting Ben. Moulton, Jo. Broderick, or Billy White, with the letter-trunk, and never were particular about the change in paying postage, so pleased were they with a letter in the well-known handwriting. Now-a-days, it would be difficult to make men, never similarly situated, understand the excitement created by the signal for a side-wheel steamer. One night "The Hunchback" was being performed at the American Theatre. C. Thorne, Senior, was "Master Walter." The house was crowded in every portion. The play had progressed to where "Julia" has quarreled with "Clifford," and "Master Walter," just hearing of it, comes in, all excitement, and walks to the centre of the stage. The actor's figure, dressed entirely in black, stood in bold relief against the white, flower-spotted scenery representing the drawing-room walls. Throwing up his arms, long and black, he exclaimed, "What does this mean?" "Side-wheel steamer," roared an immense voice from the gallery. The effect was electrical. Shouts of laughter and round upon round of applause interrupted the play for some minutes.

A little way below the Cathedral, on California street, are two old fashioned, wooden houses, of many rooms and halls, and narrow stair and passage ways, and unexpected angles, nooks and corners. Twenty years ago these houses were the aristocratic boarding-houses of the city, where dwelt Governors, Chief Justices, U. S. Land Commissioners, Commanders of the Army and Navy, and U. S. Coast Survey, lawyers of eminence, bankers and merchants, and beautiful, fashionable and accomplished ladies. The house next the Cathedral was kept by Mrs. Leland, and the other by Mrs. Petits. Neither money nor pains were spared in making comfortable the guests in these dwellings. There was an atmosphere of enjoyment, a cordial, friendly intercourse, among those who assembled at the dinner-tables, spread so bountifully there, from '49 to '56, which made very pleasant hours for the guests then, and pleasant in the recollection of to-day, with many middle-aged ladies and gentlemen.

The gentler sex were rare in those days and

accordingly worshiped, petted, feasted, courted, and constantly the recipients of costly tokens of regard from admiring acquaintances, eager for the society and humanizing influences from which California's isolation debarred them. The loveliest girl of to-day in San Francisco would open wide her eyes at the homage which was laid twenty years ago at the feet of very commonplace ladies—ladies whose school-girl days were a long way back in the perspective of life's road. The fair ones of those days, many of them, found in San Francisco fortunes as rich as the toiling miner unearthed far up in the mountains. We know, among our aristocracy of San Francisco, wealthy dames who were pretty servant girls in years gone by; one in particular, who was a nurse-maid in one of those wooden houses of which we have been writing. Neither did we ever know anything but good of them; nor do we ever meet them without feeling glad of the good fortune which is theirs.

There is a man whose face is familiar to us, and to all who frequent the business haunts, who excites a different sentiment whenever we meet him. Several years ago he was a day laborer for a man who was engaged in successful business in this city; who lived in his store, and slept there; frugal, temperate and industrious, gradually accumulating sufficient to make a home for his wife and little ones, then far away in another country. One morning his store was not opened as usual, and, upon investigation, the neighbors found him dead in his bed. It was known that the departed never had done any banking—keeping his money hidden somewhere in his premises. It could not be found; but the man in his employ, who never had any means of acquisition, save his daily wages, never sought employment elsewhere, but very soon after his employer's demise loaned several thousand dollars upon valuable improved property; and from that day to this he has been among the capitalists of San Francisco. No one is his associate. He walks the streets as if seeking something upon the pavement. His manners are morose, or spasmodically gay—plenty of money, but never a day's happiness!

Another: a large holder in a certain richly remunerative stock. He is the trustee for the property of a deceased friend's child. For years he has, by every possible means, kept from its rightful channel a large part of the constantly increasing income, diverting to his own coffers another's property. In the eyes of the business community he is one of our most respectable citizens; in his own estimation, an unhappy thief.

CHAPTER XIII.

WE were at a wedding the other evening in the Starr King Church, Rev. Dr. Stebbins, Pastor. The sight of the pretty bride made us more fully realize the flight of time, than anything that has occurred to us in our California life; because we remembered, as if it were only one year ago, the day the bride was born, and remember our taking a congratulatory glass of wine with her father. She was born on board a storeship in this harbor twenty years ago. It was very comfortable, living on a storeship in those days, and rather an enviable situation. The cabins were fitted up in the cosiest and most convenient way; there was no fear of fire, as with those ashore; no dust; and if callers were coming, they could be observed at some considerable distance in the approaching boat, and received without any inconvenience or the embarrassments incident to *deshabille* or the surprises of city life. There were many storeships then, and where they were anchored seemed a long way out in the harbor; but to-day rows of warehouses stand where the old dismasted hulks floated with their stored merchandise.

How many men now living in all the glory of soup, fish and three courses daily, from the artistic hand of a *chef*, can well remember the pie, doughnuts and coffee they took with a royal relish, at the stand in the old ship *Apollo*, on Battery street.

Two bits for a cup of coffee; two bits for a piece of pie; or if hunger and economy were to be considered, two doughnuts for a quarter of a dollar. Hardly anybody said "two bits" or quarter of a dollar in those days. It was "*dos reales!*" "*cuatro reales!*" "*un peso!*" Nearly all the new comers had either crossed the Isthmus or came by the "Horn," stopping at old Spanish cities *en route*, picking up sufficient *de la lengua* to ask for anything they wished to purchase. This coffee stand was made by cutting into the *Apollo's* hull, just under the cabin windows, and many a man who stepped ashore from his long, weary voyage, took his first meal in California at this place.

The proprietor afterwards built a commodious store for general merchandise at the corner of Battery and Sacramento streets, then the extreme end of Howison's Pier, where in honorable trade he accumulated an independence.

The men are still plentiful who like to tell of landing on the beach between Long Wharf and Jackson street; of seeing the water at very high tide, reaching to the west line of Montgomery, near the corner of Jackson street.

[*From the Alta California.*]

The old Niantic Hotel is a thing of the past—it has been torn down and carted off piecemeal. Yesterday the floor were "turned up," much to the gratification of the Micawber Convention, which has been in daily session at the corner of Clay and Sansome streets since the work of demolition commenced. The principal object of interest is the hull of the old ship *Niantic*, which formed the foundation of the building, and a portion of which is now plainly visible. The old hulk has lain there for over twenty-two years, and many old San Franciscans distincty remember the time when she was used as a storeship until the fire of May, 1851, which left nothing but the charred hull of the old vessel. The *Niantic* was an English ship, and sailed from Liverpool to Valparaiso about a quarter of a century ago. In the latter port she was purchased by Moorhead, Whitehead & Waddington, a Chilian merchant firm. They refitted the vessel and sent her to Panama, in command of Captain Cleveland. She reached that port about April, 1849, just when the California gold fever was at its height, and people were flocking from all parts of the world. The *Niantic* was at once billed for San Francisco, and in a few days after she sailed with a cargo of tropical produce and 248 passengers, arriving in this harbor on the fifth of July, 1849, after a voyage of sixty-eight days. Within a week after her arrival the crew deserted, in accordance with established usage, and the old ship was left anchored idly in the stream—a useless "elephant" on the hands of her consignees, Cook, Baker & Co. A few months later she was sold to parties here, who hauled her close in shore, near what was then the foot of Clay street, and there she has lain snugly ever since. After the May fire, in 1851, the building since known as the Niantic Hotel was erected. It was first leased by L. H. Roby (who committed suicide some two years ago), under whose management it secured the reputation of being the best hotel in the city at the time. In 1851 Roby sold out to a man named Johnson, who kept the hotel a short time, and sold out to Daniel Parrish in 1852. While Parrish kept the hotel one of his boarders was arrested on a charge of stealing a very large sum of money. He was convicted and sent to the State Prison for a term of years, but the stolen money was never recovered, although it was supposed at the time that it was secreted somewhere about the hotel, and diligent search was made for it. P. T. Woods, who had been clerking for Parrish, bought his employer out soon after the event above referred to. He did a thriving business and made money—so much, in fact, that when he settled up and "vamoosed" for parts unknown, those who knew said that he carried with him more money than he took in while "running" the Niantic Hotel.

N. H. Parkell next leased the hotel, and while he was in possession the convict one day entered the hotel office, said that he had buried a lot of money beneath the doorstep, and asked to be permitted to dig for it. Four or five feet of sand had been thrown over the place where the thief said that he had buried the money. But although it was all removed, the money was not found; and although the laborers lately engaged in pulling down the house searched diligently, it could not be found. Parkell continued the lease till 1864, when he transferred it to Miss

Mooney, sister of Assistant Engineer Con. Mooney, and she continued as landlady of the house down to the last moment of its career.

Charles L. Low is owner of the lot, and he proposes to erect forthwith a handsome and substantial four story brick building. The lower floors will be occupied by fruit and produce markets, the second story by printing-offices, and the third and fourth stories for various purposes. Having carefully stored his mind with the foregoing facts, any person will be fully qualified to mingle with the Micawbers and play himself off for an old forty-niner.

The *Niantic* storeship, at the corner of Clay and Sansome streets, was burned on the fourth of May, 1851. Upon its site the Niantic Hotel was erected, which stood until 1872, when it was torn down to make way for stores built by the owner of the land, Mr. C. L. Low. The Niantic Hotel was erected upon the ruins of the old storeship, without digging any cellar. When the excavation was made for the cellars of the new building, many relics of the fire of '51 were unearthed. The old hull at the time of the fire was imbedded in the mud some eight feet or more below the water line. At this line, after the conflagration, the *debris* was cleared away and the floor timbers of the hotel laid, covering and keeping safe from public knowledge, stowed away in the remnant of the old hull, thirty-five baskets of champagne and many other articles on storage. Twenty-one years on storage! We have not learned whether any bill for this has been sent to Mr. Van Brunt; but the wine was placed on storage by that gentleman and his partner at that time—Mr. Verplanck. Their store was on Sansome street, adjoining the *Niantic*. The wine was the *Jacquesson Fils* brand—a superior wine, very popular in California, where dry wines are always preferred. This long buried wine was found—or rather the bottles were found—in most remarkable preservation; the wires, and even the twine, being in better condition than many shipments just off the voyage from France. Champagne deteriorates after the third year; but this wine had been so completely covered as to be almost excluded from the air, and some of the wine effervesced slightly on uncorking, and was of very fair flavor.

CHAPTER XIV.

In 1849, previous to taking the house on California street, above Kearny, Mrs. Petits occupied the house standing on the spot where the Merchants' Exchange now stands, on California street, below Montgomery. The guests at this house were the leading men among the mercantile and professional class, and it was esteemed a privilege to obtain quarters there. The house stood at some distance from the street. After it was destroyed by fire, the Baron Terloo, a Russian nobleman, built two houses on this lot.

The house afterwards built on the southwest corner of Leidesdorff and California was called "The Cottage." Ellen Moon was the landlady. The adjoining house was kept by Mrs. Manning. Mrs. Moon was from Australia, and the wife or widow of an English shipmaster. The first time we saw her, she reminded us of the landlady of the "Green Dragon," in Martin Chuzzlewit; nor do we ever think of the landlady of the "Green

Dragon" now without seeing the person of Mrs. Moon. She was the personification of neatness. "There were roses in her cheeks—aye, and worth gathering, too!" This quotation—Dickens' remark upon Mrs. Lupin's appearance—came to mind the moment we saw her. The place had a cosy, comfortable air—real English—and the wines, liquors and ale in her bin needed no bush. The end and aim of her existence seemed to be somebody else's happiness and comfort, and self-abnegation. After leaving this place she opened the "Ivy Green" on Merchant street, which she kept until her death. Many who wore phylacteries upon their foreheads, and from their lofty, social pinnacle looked a long way down upon Ellen Moon, will lift their vision high as Dives' to look upon her in the world where deeds outweigh the words of Pharisees.

We have all heard of the party of miners who found an old bonnet on the road in '49, and simultaneously, without a word, dropped picks, shovels and rockers, clasped hands, as if by preconcerted signal, and capered in an amorous, laughing ring, around the cast-off head dress. We remember the day, when a woman walking along the streets of San Francisco was more of a sight than an elephant or giraffe would be to-day. Men lingered to see them pass, crowded to the wharves when they arrived, and followed them along the streets to their dwellings, and stared out of countenance the house's front. We were in Riddle's auction rooms one day, at a crowded sale, when, in a momentary pause of the auctioneer's voice, some one shouted, "Two ladies going along the sidewalk!" Instantly the crowd of purchasers rushed out, pell-mell, swarming the street so suddenly, and in such numbers, that the unconscious objects of the commotion were startled with the impression that fire or earthquake had come again.

Judge S—— told us that when he arrived in 1849, and walked up from the ship, with his wife and several little children, men crowded about the children, asking permission to kiss them, to shake hands with them, to give them gold specimens out of their chamois skin sacks, or a little gold dust to make them rings, or something for an ornament, following them a long way, as if fascinated by the sight of their child faces and voices. Mr. and Mrs. George W——, who kept a very select boarding-house on Clay street in the early days, told us of a similar experience with their children. The boys and girls of San Francisco in that time, who were not spoiled, were remarkable children. The sight of their faces touched tender places in the hearts of men, divided by a continent's breadth from their own little ones; and to give other children toys, money, or something for their happiness, was a natural impulse, however questionable as to ultimate results.

When the Custom House, on the corner of California and Montgomery, was destroyed by the fire of May 4th, 1851, the treasure saved in the brick vault was removed to the bank of Palmer, Cook & Co., corner of Washington and Kearny. A guard, *a la militaire*, composed of the Custom House officials, armed and equipped, under the command of T. Butler King, Collector, escorted the revenue money from the ruins of the Custom House to the bank, "in due and ancient form." This action of the Collector excited much ridicule and many newspaper squibs, and brought forth a comic ode, satirical of T. Butler King. To those well informed upon the numbers, character and proceedings of the professional burglars, murderers and thieves infesting San Francisco, the action of the Collector in guarding so thoroughly the Government money entrusted to him, was laudable and praiseworthy in the highest degree.

We remember that while the Custom House boys were standing in the street awaiting the opening of the vault, Captain Macondray, who happened in the neighborhood, said: "Well, boys, suppose we go over to the 'Blue Wing,' and join in a universal drink, before the army takes up its line of march?"

Tom Harvey replied: "The motion is in order," and George Bromley said: "So mote it be!" and the Captain's hospitable offer was carried into effect. This "universal drink" was a favorite expression of the Captain's, when offering hospitality to any numerous gathering. All the residents of that time knew Captain Macondray, his kind face and welcome smile, his sparkling eye and short, curling hair, his compact figure, and the firm, honest grasp of his hand.

One of the familiar objects of San Francisco was Captain Macondray on his black, pacing horse, a sleek, easy-moving nag, with four white feet. Erect in his saddle, his gray, felt hat, with the rim caught up close against the crown each side, *a la chapeau militaire*—moving about in all the business streets, the Captain's face and form were ever pleasant to the eyes of his fellow-citizens then, as now is the memory of his sterling virtues.

The old signal station on Telegraph Hill was a very important feature in the days when those long, black arms stretched out to tell thousands of anxious husbands, fathers and lovers that the steamer, bearing news of hope and happiness, or of the death of loved ones, was then in sight. How that signal for a "side-wheel" (the mails were brought only on the side-wheel steamers)— how it did wake up the street! All along the line of stores were men out upon the walk, their faces all turned in one direction, looking at the signal. They couldn't do any business after a sight at those well-known, outstretched, uplifted arms, almost human in their welcome significance. "Come in, bye and bye!" the merchant would say to his customer; "the steamer is telegraphed!" "What!" (with delighted surprise); "didn't know that!" and the would-be buyer left in a hurry. The idea of news from wife, children or sweetheart to a man, thirty days' distance away, made him ignore business at once.

The old telegraph-station was a place of much resort. It was attractive from its associations, and it was good exercise to walk up there, and the view repaid the trouble. There were good, generous, refreshing milk-punches to be had in the room beneath the look-out on the roof, where privileged visitors could ascend and use the telescope. Without a telescope, to-day, it will be very interesting to any man who knew San Francisco twenty years ago—yes, ten years ago—to walk up to the hill-top and "view the landscape o'er." There are thousands of men in San Francisco who have not been to the summit of Telegraph Hill in eighteen years, nor will our eloquence coax them to attempt it; but it is really worth the trouble.

Mr. Bradley (now of Bradley & Rulofson), the daguerrean—there were no photographers in those days—practised his art on the west side of Montgomery, between Washington and Jackson. His prices were from eight dollars upwards, according to the size and style of the portrait and frame. The courteous artist was hardly allowed time to breathe, much less to eat, or take a moment's rest for a day or two before the departure of a steamer. Californians were so anxious that their friends in civilized countries should see just how they looked in their mining dress, with their terrible revolver, the handle protruding menacingly from the holster, somehow, twisted in front, when sitting for a daguerreotype to send "to the States." They were proud of their curling moustaches and flowing beards; their bandit-looking *sombreros;* and our old friend Bradley accumulated much *oro en polvo,* and many yellow coins from the private mints of Wass, Molitor & Co., Moffatt & Co., Dubosque, and Baldwin & Co. Mr. Bradley appears just the same to-day (at Bradley & Rulofson's) as he did twenty-three years ago; wears the same conventional silk hat, so seldom seen in those days—so universally worn now; the same quiet black suit; and his hair and beard were almost as silvery then as now. Neither has he altered in the urbanity and unvarying courtesy which made him so popular and filled his purse twenty-three years ago. Many of the old daguerreotypes and ambrotypes are preserved by those to whom they were sent; and many a middle-aged husband and father has had them carelessly handed to him by his wife or the big boys and girls, in the secret, who were much amused at his questions, and failure in recognizing Mr. Bradley's production, of which he was so proud so many years ago.

John S. Eagan's paint, oil and varnish store was on Montgomery street, two or three doors north of the Custom House. Mr. Eagan was a very prominent member of Howard Engine Co., and was enthusiastic in every thing for public good or private charity, and never hesitated about putting his hand in his pocket and giving liberally on the slightest provocation. Bob. Bernard used to paint signs and fancy work for Eagan, and it was quite a pleasure to watch his steady hand and rapid progress with the brush and pencil. He used to stand off from his work, holding his brush at arm's length, drawing the color along the lines, plumb up to the angles of the letters, as easily, and calmly, and exactly, without pause, tremor or hesitation, as if uncertainty or nervousness were something entirely unknown to him. It was a treat to see him sweep his pencil on the curves of great, street-sign letters as gracefully and easily as if he were waving a signal, or giving from the leader's stand, to an orchestra, the *tempo* for an adagio movement. Mr. Bernard worked so easily and so rapidly, that his salary for the week's effort was little, if any less, than that of the President of the United States for an equal period. Fires were so frequent then, and the gambling-saloons so spacious, so elaborately decorated and gilded every time they were rebuilt—so many new business firms were forming and changing, requiring new signs and numbers, that Messrs. Eagan and Bernard accumulated money in a most interesting manner. They were not "Eagan & Bernard" as a firm, although they were in the same store, and worked for each other's interest much better than partners in business generally do.

CHAPTER XV.

Lieut. Derby ("John Phœnix"), U. S. A., was standing in Barry & Patten's doorway, then No. 116 Montgomery street, one pleasant morning, when, raising his grave, thoughtful eyes, he saw a horse and wagon passing by, navigated by a phlegmatic Teuton. "Eagle Bakery" was inscribed in heavy capitals upon the vehicle.

"Hi! hallo you!" exclaimed Derby. The countryman of "Our Fritz" slowly turned his stolid gaze upon the lieutenant, who was beckoning so earnestly, that the driver hauled up, slowly turned his horse around to the curbstone, and inquired: "Vat you vants?" "I'll take a baked eagle!" said Phœnix. "Eh? vat ish dat?" said the sleepy-headed fellow. "A baked eagle! don't you understand?" said Phœnix, with feigned impatience. "I pakes pread!" said the indignant *deutscher*, preparing to drive on. "Stop!" said Derby, in an authoritative voice. "You're an imposter! How dare you deceive the public in this way? Here have I been for six weeks trying to get a baked eagle, which my medical adviser prescribes for my health, and you have raised hopes only to deceive me. Now, listen! if you don't have those words—that falsehood, painted out immediately, I'll have you put under arrest and court-martialed! Away!" He 'waved the astonished, adopted citizen from his august presence; and he was not slow to go, as he had evidently, from the appearance of his widened mouth and eyes, taken the affair as a serious matter.

Many people have the impression that Lieut. Derby was a devotee of Bacchus, and we have heard it said that he was a very dissipated man. We know that in our acquaintance with him, from '51 to the time of his being ordered East, we never saw him put to his lips a glass of wine, ale or spirits, or anything that could intoxicate. We have been much in his company, and under all kinds of circumstances, where the weakness would have "cropped out" had it been latent, but a strong lemonade was the extent of his libations, in all the time we knew him.

When Derby graduated from West Point, he was one morning in the office, at the headquarters of the army, in Washington. Gen. H——, one of the oldest officers in the army, a venerable, white-haired soldier, was seated at his desk, engaged in conversation upon some official business. Upon its conclusion, he turned to the young cadet, a big lad, and greeted him with a very pleasant "Good morning, Mr. Derby, happy to see you, sir! take a seat." Derby sat down, bowing his acknowledgments, with the demure look he often assumed. "Anything new?" asked the General. "Well, no, sir!—nothing particular, excepting that remarkable gun, invented by Captain ———, of the artillery," said the young graduate modestly, looking into his cap, which he was diffidently twirling in his hands. "What gun? I have heard nothing about it!" said the General, with awakening interest. "Please describe it!" Several officers of various grades and rank, present at the time, were listening attentively. Derby arose, placed his cap upon the chair, looked towards the table where drawing materials were lying, modestly requesting permission to illustrate the principle of the new gun. The General eagerly acquiesced. Derby, who was quite facile with the pencil, rapidly sketched a diagram of the gun, surrounded all the time by interested auditors. "Now, sir," said the unassuming but talented young engineer, holding up before the old General his neat and lucid drawing: "This is Captain ———'s invention for throwing projectiles in a curved line, to sweep them around and behind intervening objects." The General, who had been scrutinizing the illustration with the utmost attention, now turned the most searching look upon the speaker's earnest, modest and serious face. Derby clearly and succinctly explained the principle of the weapon, the shape of the projectile, its motion and effect, thus and so. Letter A, the muzzle of the gun; letter B, the line describing the flight of the destructive missile, its course, and so on. His language was so fluent, the words so clear and distinct, his use of artillery terms betraying such great intelligence upon the subject, that his listeners, not quite grasping the idea, charged their obtuseness to ignorance upon the subject.

"Has the principle been tested?" inquired the General, when the young subaltern had ceased. "Yes, sir; Sergeant McCue fired the gun off yesterday morning." "What was the result?" "The shot passed entirely around the barracks, striking the gunner in the *os coccyges*." The veteran officer turned square upon the speaker, that he might see him more directly through his spectacles—like one who doubted his sense of hearing. There was a breathless silence, while the oldest General in the army was reading the blank, puzzling face of the youngest graduate of West Point.

A General *was* a General twenty years ago, and consternation was on every soldier's face; but, to the great relief of all, the General burst out with a hearty laugh, which was joined in by every one. "Mr. Derby!" said the lenient old soldier, placing his hand gently upon the young scapegrace's shoulder, "remember that it is only once in a man's lifetime, and under peculiar circumstances, that such a thing would be overlooked." And it is reasonable to believe that no other individual in all the army could, under the circumstances, have had immunity.

A real "London-cry" candy man held forth in the early days on the west side of Montgomery, near Clay street. His little shop-on-wheels displayed its store of sweets, over which he waxed eloquent. His sonorous voice rang out, with a distinct and banging emphasis, that would not be ignored. He was something of a humorist, and made good local hits, going on with the most serious voice and grave face; his head lifted, but with downcast eyes, like one exhorting against time, for a good salary. His tall, black, narrow-rimmed hat could never have been built off English territory; his precise cravat and unrelenting shirt-collar were cockney; his telling tone and clear pronunciation, vaunting his goods, betrayed a long experience: "Hore-hound—Pep-per-mint—and —Win-ter-green! Large lumps! and strong-ly fla-vored!" A short, dead pause, and "'Ere they go!" This was three times given in a tone to excite the envy of a drill-sergeant or a stump-speaker; occasionally diversified with the assertion that Judge ———— bought them; that Col. ———— bought them; always naming some prominent individual. One evening he amused the public by exclaiming, in a voice of unusual power: "Buy 'em up! Every body buys 'em! Tom B—tt—e's sweetheart buys 'em! 'Ere they go!" Busy-bodies lost no time in informing Tom of the distinction forced upon him. He strolled along, listening. Out it rang upon the air. Watching an opportunity to speak, unheard by others, he walked up quickly, saying, "Look here! you quit that, or I'll horsewhip you!" "All right!" said the itinerant in a soft voice—so unlike those vociferous lungs, bowing low and courteously; then, straightening up, he roared out in the well-known voice, "Tom B—tt—e's sweetheart does *not* buy 'em!!" Tom looked uneasily around. The horsewhip threat wouldn't work; there was a rapid and evidently satisfactory consultation. T. B—— had undoubtedly concluded, as many men since that day have also believed, that when prominent men are possessed of the public ear, and—*little facts*—'twere best to subsidize. Whatever were the terms of that whispered compact, the obnoxious utterance was never heard again.

The figure, dress, and especially the hat of the candy man, calls to our memory the fancy coachman and his stunning carriage and pair— a real English turnout, the hired possession of which, for an hour or two, almost led a man into the belief that he was more than the self-same individual on foot—that he surely must have been intended by Nature for the occupant of that equipage, despite Fortune's shortcomings. The driver, horses and carriage came from Australia, and took up their position on the southeast corner of the Plaza and Kearny street. The driver was the most conventionally correct type of an English coachman, possible to imagine. His sleek, tall, black hat, drab coat of many capes, his spick-span gauntlets, his whip, and the *technique* of its position upon his knee, with his hand clasped upon its long handle, just above the polished rings, reminded one of a king of England, sitting on his throne, with sceptre-handle resting on the royal knee, as represented in our childhood's picture books. It was such a wonderful thing to ride behind this dignitary; to make calls or " shop," hedged round by such a tower of strength; so like " Pa's carriage," and not the least odor of a hired hack. Ten dollars an hour, if engaged three hours, or more; fifteen dollars per hour for two hours; and twenty for the single hour. Seldom was he idle. He made his turnout so attractive that patrons felt satisfied, and he never wanted for custom. We believe that, as a rule, those who, seeking public support, perform their part better than any other, get their reward. The coachman of our sketch most surely did, for he purchased a wholesome bill of exchange on "the old lady of Threadneedle street" when he left for home.

CHAPTER XVI.

There were a number of little public houses, of the lowest order and worst reputation, scattered about on the hillside, bounded by the lines of Montgomery, Kearny, Pacific and Broadway, and still higher up the hill, in 1849, '50 and '51. Shabby little dens, with rough, hangdog fellows lounging about their doorways; fellows with their features concealed by slouched hats; fellows who always had a way of sliding out of sight when you looked at them, as if they were averse to looking any one in the eye. Skulking knaves, shunning observation in the daylight, but very inquisitive after dark, coming close up to the passer-by, with an effrontery of persistent, impudent curiosity, very disconcerting to the timid or unarmed, benighted citizen. Nearly, or quite, all of these *cribs* were kept by Sydney men and women of the lowest class. The signs, swinging or nailed above the doors, were the old, historical, English or Scotch public-house names, found all over Great Britain and Australia. The familiar ale-house names, "The Magpie," "The Bobby Burns," "The Boar's Head," "The Bird in Hand," "The Jolly Waterman," "Tam O'Shanter," "The Bay of Biscay," and such time-honored inn names. The man whose path happened to pass these places after night fall, in those days when the way was all unevenness and darkness, the hill-side steep and toilsome, no lights, and the neighborhood with very few respectable dwellings, did not feel as safe as when upon the populous streets below. If his step were firm and regular, if he carried his head up and went bravely on his way, his steps were dogged but a short distance. If the skulking follower were suddenly confronted, and heard the sharp, ominous *click, click!* he "vanished like a ghost at cock-crow;" but woe to the purse, if not the person, of the unlucky man who came that way oblivious of his whereabouts, his watchfulness lulled, and napping, by reason of potent and deep libations. Many a man came to consciousness at daylight, lying chilled and benumbed on the damp hillside, with his head in an agony of fiery pain, unable to bridge the impenetrable chasm of the past few hours; the only gleam of light upon the situation, dawning upon him through the discovery that his money, watch, knife and pistol—every article of value he remembered having on his person when last conscious—were gone. The sand-bag weapon of assassination is silent, sudden and deadly, unless the robber be merciful—cares only for the money, not the life—happens to be in good humor, and does not strike maliciously. The sand-bag is sure death, if the blow be heavy, leaving no outward mark, no fracture, no trickling blood or swelled abrasion. It jars the brain to utter and eternal oblivion. "*Found dead—no marks of violence—apoplexy the supposed cause,*" was not an unfrequent notice in the *Alta* and *Herald* of those days.

MacClaren's Hotel, on the little lane leading from Mission—just where the residence of Geo. Wright used to stand, now Woodward's Garden —through to Folsom street, was a cozy, quiet, sleepy little public house, built close against sand-hills, rising higher than its roof, sheltering it from the north and west winds, as it stood facing the south and basking in the fervent sunlight, just midway in the sandy path between the streets, and sufficiently remote to lose the noisy rumble of the carriages on both. A jolly place to lounge in easy, ricketty, old China cane chairs and on bulgy old sofas, with one's hat tipped down over face and eyes, shutting out the sun's light, while feeling its warm, revitalizing comfort stealing through every nerve and bone in the sleepy body, and no sudden clatter of hoofs or rattling carriage wheels dashing up to disturb one's somnolent enjoyment. The roadway of the lane was sandy and dry in some places, and in others, a little, lazy brook crept across, smoothing and wetting it like the sea beach; and as you sat, dozing away the hours, idle, for the time, 'tis true, but, imbibing at every pore a fresh stock of life and strength for future labors, the voices of new comers reached your ear before the tramping of their horses' hoofs, muffled by the soft sand; and the impulse to get into a dignified, sitting posture gave way, sleepily, to the question, "From which direction are they coming?"

You were quite sure they were from the Mission road, when first you heard them, and lifted back your hat just enough to blink a little at the trees skirting that portion of the lane; but the effort was too much — the bright sunlight dancing through the reticulated stems and leaves, was quite confusing to your long-shaded eyes, and you drew down your sheltering *sombrero*, and sank back again to muse upon it. You dropped asleep in a second's time, and in the same time woke again, fully impressed with the belief that hours had passed since you fell off, while waiting to see who they were—those people coming down the lane from the Mission road-end, and—very curious—there they were! right upon the ground before the house, but from the Folsom street way. Rousing and vainly endeavoring to solve the problem, whether it was MacClaren's beer, or the Stilton, that had made you "lose yourself"—you observe that the guests, laughing and chatting so merrily, are George Aiken, Charley Rebello and Captain Maryatt, three vivacious young Britishers, all well mounted and good horsemen.

They do not permit you to doze in the sun during their stay. At sight of them Mac hails his spouse, who quickly appears with cold meats, pickles and relishes, an old English cheese, butter, and a big, home-made loaf, while Mac commences opening beer—not one bottle, but many—long, yellow-labelled bottles of Allsopp. What an appetite for beer, and for bread and cheese, too, those young Englishmen had in those days; and as to that matter, their American cousins were not very slow, in those bright days of youth, health, hope and unsophisticated stomachs. What a wonderful incentive to eating, is the air of California, and how good the bread and butter used to be at MacClaren's! Good butter in those days was a rare thing. Many people used to ride out to Mac's just to eat the scarce delicacy. They would become indignant at their sour French bread or stereotyped German loaf, and firkin butter, *via* Panama, worked over in lime-water, stamped in little pats, and sworn to as fresh ranch butter; and thinking of the sweet, fresh, cool, genuine luxury, and the great, crisp, brown, home-made English loaf, always to be found at Mac's, they would straightway march to the nearest stable and hire a saddle horse or vehicle, to make the quickest time for that cozy, old, English public-house, now gone the way of all mortality.

William Vincent Wallace, the highly gifted composer of "Maritana," was in San Francisco in its early days. The precise time of his arrival from Australia we never knew, nor the date of his departure for New York; but we are sure that he was in the latter place very early in 1853. Wallace came every day while in San Francisco, to an ale-house on California street, very near where now is the office of the Spring Valley Water Works Co. The ale-house was kept by an Englishman named Jackson, a man of culture, taste and talent, and something of an artist. He molded a little plaster medallion of Wallace's head in profile, an artistic production, and a good likeness. Wallace, as we remember him, was about five feet eight inches in height; a round, white, high forehead, and nearly bald upon the crown, but the rest of his well-shaped head plentifully clothed with light brown, almost flaxen hair. He wore the English style of side whiskers, but no moustache or imperial; his weight must have been near one hundred and seventy pounds.

It is said that Wallace was an Irishman, and we are quite certain that he was, although his appearance was that of a Scotchman or blonde Britisher. His manner was reticent, save with congenial people, but quietly affable at all times. Wallace's wife died in San Francisco, and was buried in Happy Valley, which seemed at that time more remote than the Lone Mountain of to-day. Happy Valley was frequently a place of sepulture prior to the establishment of Yerba Buena cemetery; but the spot where all those dead, still sleep, can now be no more pointed out, than the blue ocean wave, which once opened to receive its dead, gently enfolding and concealing them forever.

In the second story of Macondray & Co's

store, corner of Sansome and Pine, were sleeping apartments for members of the firm and clerks in the house. One afternoon towards dusk, Tom Cary, who had been posting books in one of the up-stairs rooms, where he might not be disturbed, came out of the room towards the stairway descending to the main store, when he noticed Belcher Kay's head, just above the edge of the floor around the staircase. Kay, who was taking a rapid survey of the interior, started in a confused way, saying "Ah, how d'ye do?—rooms up-stairs, eh?—do people sleep up here?—nice place, eh?" "Yes, Belcher," said Mr. Cary, in a pointed way, "there are several men sleep up here, and they are always well armed; and we have watchmen, and dogs that do not sleep in case the watchman should happen to." The tone of this reply was too significant not to be understood by Belcher, who simply said, "Ah, just so. Good evening, Mr. Cary," and withdrew.

Kay, who had been elected to the office of Port Warden for San Francisco, and treated with much kindness by gentlemen who were formerly pupils in his school for the art of self defense, had failed to appreciate it, returning to his old ways, and association with thieves and burglars, as subsequent events verified. He was assisted by a *confrere* from Boston in his escape. The day we came ashore in San Francisco, we were walking with a friend who came on our ship, and who at home was a pupil at Kay's gymnasium. Kay was delighted to see one of his old scholars, and asked, as a great favor, if he would go down to his boat—Kay was the Port Warden then—and make a few notes for him, as he had injured his right hand and was unable to hold a pencil. The whilom pupil at once consented, and we went off aboard the ship. Kay issued his orders, which were duly noted down by the impromptu clerk, who soon came ashore. When we were alone, he laughed, saying, "You didn't understand that dodge!" "What is it?" "Nothing; only Kay never could write."

In the month of January, '51, or perhaps some time earlier, in the last of '50, Mr. Nathaniel Page was unloading some lumber on the beach, between Sacramento and California streets, as near as we can remember, about where Halleck street joins Leidesdorff. While giving his orders to the workmen engaged, Mr. Page was peremptorily ordered to remove that lumber and vacate the premises. Looking around at the person so dictatorial, Mr. Page saw Captain

Folsom gesticulating violently; and before any explanation could be made, the Captain drew his revolver and fired at Mr. Page. The shot struck the watch in the latter's pocket, hitting it with a slant, glancing off, and perforating the side of a boat about fifty feet distant. Mr. Page wore his watch in the waistband pocket of his pants, as was the fashion in those days, and a very fortunate thing for Mr. Page that it was the fashion just at that moment. The occurrence attracted some attention and a little gathering at the moment, otherwise no notice was taken of it. Might was right in those days, and Captain Folsom was very arbitrary and dictatorial, by reason of his position and the funds at his command, and was accustomed to immediate obedience. He was a generous, impulsive man, but too hasty on this occasion, having no reason to fear any squatter pretension from Mr. Page, who was as good a citizen as lived in the community; and, we are pleased to say, that we consider him such at the present writing. Pistols were very freely used by hot-headed people in early days. Captain Folsom, we know, was ashamed of his conduct, for he afterward dealt largely in a business way with the man whose life he had endangered.

CHAPTER XVII.

STARKEY, JANION & Co's store was on the southwest corner of California and Sansome streets. It stood in an enclosure with gates. The building was two stories, with a steep, sloping roof, and had a balcony or veranda around the second story. The building was painted white, and the posts and rails of the veranda were painted green. The building in those days seemed quite substantial and spacious. In the evening, after business hours, the gates were closed, all snug and secluded, when ruddy-faced, portly men might be seen leisurely pacing the balcony, smoking their No. 1 Manilas, suggestive of men who had dined well, and drank good old port with dessert; comfortable looking men, the sight of whom would excite the envy of some passer-by, who had "dined with Duke Humphrey." The fire swept away this house, leaving no vestige of the comfortable looking composite of store, counting house and residence.

West of Starkey, Janion & Co's store, on the south side of California street, were the stores of Glen & Co., Backus & Harrison, S. H. Williams & Co., DeBoum, Vigneaux & Grisar, and G. B. Post & Co.

After the fire of June 14th, 1850, J. L. Riddle & Co. built an extensive shanty of China matting, wisely concluding that if conflagrations were to be so frequent, it were better to raise a mere shelter for their goods, at the least possible expense.

The building occupied by this firm prior to the fire of June 14th, was a substantial three story wooden store on Sacramento street, north side, just above the corner of Leidesdorff. The upper story of this building was used as a dormitory for all the acquaintances of the firm who wished to sleep there—ship masters who happened to be late ashore—new arrivals who had not established themselves—any man or boy who knew Riddle & Co. It was a spacious room, nearly square. Hammocks were slung at every corner and available post. All about the room were cots, stretchers and mattresses, plenty of blankets and pillows, but no sheets or pillow-cases.

Against the walls on all sides were large China water-jars, China wash-stands and large

China-stone wash-basins, and cocoanut-shell dippers. Nearly all the furniture then was of China importation; and very commodious, stylish and comfortable it was, too. The man who went early to bed in this apartment, might sleep undisturbed until midnight or a little after; but about that time, several young men, not long from Boston, would return from protracted meetings—young men musically inclined, who wished to rehearse just once more before retiring. These birds of Minerva would sometimes discover that a sleeper had possession of a very comfortable place they fancied for themselves, which would cause a playful argument on the sleeper's right of possession. When Judge Blackburn, Bob Parker and Charley Southard were in town, Riddle & Co's hospitable roof sheltered them, and they were not disposed to sleep, as long as any fun could be got out of anybody or anything.

Judge Blackburn would have a wrestling match with Charley Southard, and as the Judge was about six feet four and Charley about four feet six, it was considered rather unequal, and excited lively comments from the aroused and thoroughly interested fellow-lodgers. Bets were freely offered by Jim Riddle, Eben Niles, Ward Eaton, Jim Leighton, Harry Spiel, *et al.*

Some one would throw a pillow, or a light cane chair, or some harmless thing, to trip up the contestants, which roused the ire of some one else who had a wager pending; then there was a general hullabaloo, and pelting of pillows, mattresses, china cushions, etc., a perfect pandemonium. There were no ladies or children to disturb; nothing that the fellows did seemed to hurt them; their heads and stomachs seemed stronger than copper, and sleep was almost ignored.

Captain Charley Scholfield was always to be seen at Riddle & Co's in the day time; he had a little house of his own—his "ranch," as he liked to call it. He was a very eccentric man; affected the nautical, bluff style, interspersing his remarks very freely with emphatic expletives, and assuming a rough deportment entirely foreign to his nature, for he was all gentleness and kindness. He always wore a full suit of navy blue, prim, plain and old-fashioned, a brown vicuna hat, never changing the style, as the city changed and '49 customs gradually vanished. He clung to everything belonging to the days when everybody was free and easy, liberal and unconventional, and gradually disappeared from his old haunts—or, perhaps, they disappeared from him—and he lived almost in seclusion, in his little box on Post street, next to the large lot on which Alcalde Hyde's house stood. Here, to the last, he lived as they used to live in the pioneer days; his little single cot and blankets, the big China water-jar—its cover a piece of redwood, with a nail in the centre for a handle—the cocoanut-shell dipper; a demijohn under the table; clean glasses on the table—the Captain was scrupulously neat—and a box of cigars on the shelf, welcome to all who had the *open sesame* of an early *residente*. It is many years since the Captain went the way of all good pioneers; but many are left who will recognize his peculiarities recalled by our sketch.

The fire of June 14th, 1850, smoked out the *habitues* of Riddle & Co's upper story, and most of them went to the rooms over Mr. Hoff's store, on the extreme end of Howison's Pier, which was crowded with goods of every description, saved from the fire. Close against Mr. Hoff's store was a large quantity of clothing—black dress suits. The morning after the fire, we were all standing on the pier, looking at the ruins of the city, when a pleasant, black-eyed little man, with an aquiline nose—a brisk little man, who had been standing thoughtfully looking at the goods on the pier, and many suits lying in the mud, where they had been crowded off the pier—suddenly came up to us and said: "Gentlemen, if any of those clothes will fit any of you, help yourselves! You are quite welcome to them; there's no place to store them, and they'll be ruined here. I shall enter them on my books as *closed out by fire!*" We all stared at him, when he commenced talking to us, supposing him demented by losses or over-exertion at the fire, and want of sleep; but the good sense of his remarks was quite convincing; very much so to men just relieved of their wardrobes, and we were not slow in returning thanks and availing ourselves of the kind offer. Shortly after, the entire party looked as if they were ready for church, soiree or funeral. For years after this incident it was a standing remark with all of them, meeting any one of the number with new clothes, to say: "Ah! where was the fire?"

It was considered the correct thing, among the men of that time, to help themselves to a clean shirt from the collection of the friend under whose roof night had overtaken them. There was a discrepancy, of course, when host and guest were greatly different in stature; but little things like that were not of any moment in those exciting, prosperous days. The long-limbed man sometimes had to coax the wristbands of his short friend's shirt, and the short-necked individual's ears were sometimes in danger from the stiff-starched collar of his long-necked, hospitable friend. The laundry clerk who did not mark with care each lot of linen, could never have sorted them by sizes; while it was nothing strange for a man to find only one or two shirts that would fit him, out of his clean dozen from the laundry.

Captain Gillespie was the wharfinger at Long Wharf (a very short wharf it was really) in 1850. Young Eddy was the assistant wharfinger, and young O'Brien the gate-clerk. Capt. Gillespie is now in an insurance office in New York. Mr. Eddy was afterwards in Newhall & Gregory's auction and commission-house, and subsequently was Quartermaster in the U. S. Army. He perished in the calamity which befel the steamer *Brother Jonathan*, off our northern coast. Gen. Wright and wife, and Capt. Chaddock, of the U. S. Revenue Service, were lost on board the same vessel. The engines which were on this ill-fated steamer urged to destruction the *Atlantic* and her doomed passengers on Long Island Sound, many long years before.

The late Harry Isaacs succeeded Capt. Gillespie as wharfinger, and subsequently was proprietor of the "Identical," where Hussey, Bond & Hale were located, previous to building on Sansome, near California.

Capt. David Scannell, late Chief Engineer of the San Francisco Fire Department, came to California in 1850. He was captain of a New York company in the war with Mexico, and was in every battle, from the Rio Grande to the city of Mexico, behaving with the utmost gallantry in every engagement. He was Sheriff of San Francisco at a time when all his surroundings were of a nature to prejudice the public against him; but he never, knowingly, touched a dishonest dollar in his life. We were once of a widely different opinion; but for the past seventeen years have had constant opportunities to note that he is always an efficient officer, a punctiliously honorable man, ever a peacemaker—full of charity and kindness. We are pleased to record this of a man to whom great injustice was done in the community, but of whom one estimate only can exist in the minds of those who really and truly know him.

Hussey, Bond & Hale were on Howison's Pier in 1850, and subsequently on Sansome street, near the southwest corner of California. Mr. Bond was more a resident of New York than

San Francisco. Messrs. Hussey and Hale were the resident partners here. The latter filled the office of City Auditor for many years, with honor to himself, and satisfaction to his fellow-citizens. As a business man and an accountant, Mr. Henry M. Hale has had few equals in California. For many years Mr. Hale was the business manager of the San Francisco Sugar Refining Co., and confidential secretary of the late George Gordon.

Mr. James Laidley was on Commercial street in August, 1850. He erected a house there, as soon as the new extension of the street was completed from Montgomery to Kearny. It was a frame house, made and fitted in Philadelphia, and brought to San Francisco on the ship *Wm. V. Kent*. Mr. Laidley shipped another house from Philadelphia on the *Algoma*. The latter house was erected on First street, nearly opposite Donahue's foundry, and was called "The Isthmus." It was kept as a lodging-house by a Mr. Haste. The accommodations were open bunks, in rows or tiers, along each side of the room, and a double row in the centre. The couch draperies were gray blankets and pillows, minus the linen cases, or any other cases, for which luxuries one dollar per night was the charge. Mr. Laidley was the owner, but not interested in the business of either of the houses. Whatever Mr. Laidley does interest himself in, is very effectually carried out, and a truer friend or more liberal man never came to California.

J. C. Flood and W. S. O'Brien were living on the corner of Pacific and Mason streets in 1849–50, boarding at Mr. Parker's house. Whether they were "Flood & O'Brien" then, as a business firm or not, we cannot say; but they were friends, and have been no less so in all the years of business partnership—that crucible-like test of character and friendship. Mr. O'Brien we remember as dealing in produce, a very profitable business early in '50. Afterwards, we think, he kept the United States Hotel. Some years after this time we knew Mr. Flood as Flood & O'Brien, on Washington street, near Sansome, and have always found him very like his partner—an unassuming, amiable man, always prompt, shrewd and correct in business.

CHAPTER XVIII.

In the early days of San Francisco, men were not in the least fastidious about their occupation. Young gentlemen of elegant leisure in the older cities, scholars just graduated from college, boys just away from the counting-house desk, attracted hither by the golden stories, took hold manfully at rough laborers' work. There is to-day a banker on Montgomery street, who stepped upon the beach in San Francisco with only half a dollar in his pocket, in the early part of 1849, then a boy less than nineteen years of age. He had a letter to a prominent man in the city, but was too sensitive to present it. While standing, thinking what to do, he was accosted by a man, who said, " Want to go to work for an hour or two?" " Yes, sir," eagerly answered the boy, following, with no more words. His first work in California was to assist another young fellow, who stood waiting, to remove a pile of lumber to make way for the foundation of a new store. This job lasted a couple of hours, for which he received five dollars. Elated by his first endeavor and its good remuneration, he walked farther up the hill (it was a gradual rise then from the beach to the top of Clay street hill) until he reached the Plaza (Portsmouth Square), where he halted to observe some men digging for the foundation of the Parker House.

After standing a few minutes, he was hailed by the foreman: "Want to work?" "Yes, sir." "Come on; here's a shovel!" This paid him well. The next job was a good long one, lightering coal, which, when finished, left money enough in his pocket to start a fruit and pea-nut stand on the Plaza, which paid him a nice little sum daily. One day, a man came up to his stand, called him by name, and shook his hand cordially. It was one of the firm in whose store he had commenced life after leaving school. The new comer, just landed and unsophisticated, asked, "Wouldn't you rather be at work in the old store again?" "No thank'e, sir," said the boy, "I'm clearing every day more than I used to receive in a month in the old store."

Another old resident, who has houses and lands to-day, was standing on Montgomery street, near Clay, wishing to begin work in his new home, when a man came to the door of the store where our friend stood, and said, "Look here, my friend, if you won't get mad about it, I'll offer you a dollar to fill that box with sand." "Thank you," said the young fellow, "I'll fill it all day long on those terms, and never become angry in the least." "All right! take it right out there, where they are hauling sand for grading." The box, about as large as an ordinary claret case, was filled, brought to the store, and the dollar was paid. "Now," said the recipient, "We'll go and take a drink with this dollar, if you please." His new employer laughingly acquiesced, which led to the new comer's employment in the store where his first dollar was earned, until the fire of May 4th, 1851, and a good connection until the present day.

There is a man now in this city who made forty thousand dollars as carrier of the *Alta California* newspaper; and another who realized thirty thousand dollars carrying the Sacramento *Union* and San Francisco *Evening Bulletin*. These cases are personally known to us; and another of a washerwoman, whose earnings, early invested in real estate, give her to-day a property worth $100,000. A magnate in real estate, who may be seen daily on Montgomery street, formerly peddled potatoes along the same streets where now his own buildings

"Rear their tall arches towering to the sky."

Finding a man engaged in his own trade or profession—the work for which he had been educated—was a rare thing in California. Delicately nurtured men were doing the work of common laborers. Young students, whose biceps knew only the gymnasium's development, who had handled nothing heavier than a fencing foil, or mottled malacca, grew familiar with the shovel, pick and rocker. San Francisco wrought many anomalous conditions in life. The whilom professor of a Maryland College was a drayman on Pacific Wharf. Graduates of Yale and Harvard, however they construed Horace or Virgil, were guilty of no false quantities in their symposiac compositions. The once wealthy money broker of State street, Boston, chopped wood and tended fires for a baker's oven.

The young lawyer who, from lack of clients, peddled port-monnaies in Marysville, could have lost nothing of his legal acumen in the itinerant departure, as he has since then sat as Associate Judge on the United States Supreme Bench. One of a prominent law firm in San Francisco is no worse an advocate because of his experience as waiter in a popular restaurant.

Nor do we think that the gentleman who once filled the office of County Recorder, with satisfaction to the citizens and honor to himself, ever regrets the skill which he, an amateur violinist, acquired during his professional experience, at twenty dollars *per diem* in one of the temples of chance on the Plaza, in the spring of '50.

Judge ———, an able jurist, now occupying the bench of an interior district, found himself in California in 1849, without money, clients, chambers, or a brief. Being something of a gastronomist, he accepted the post of *chef* in a restaurant. One morning, while engaged in preparing the day's edibles, a stranger looked in at the kitchen door, nodded, and wished the Judge "Good morning!"

"*Buenos dias!*" said the Judge—everybody attempted a little Spanish in those days—and they were soon in conversation. Everybody was social then—good-natured and happy, because they were prosperous; there's nothing so conducive to good temper and honesty, as prosperity.

"I've got a case up here in Court," said the stranger, "and I don't know 'zactly what to do about it." "What is the case?" asked the Judge, interested at once. "Tell me the facts."

"Well," said the other, "you see it's just this way. I shipped a lot of goods for this place, and the ship's arrived, and her cargo all discharged, and my goods ain't nowhere." "Have you the papers you received from the office where you shipped your goods?" "Oh, yes, every one of 'em. Here they are." The Judge neglected the *chef's* duty, and carefully examined the documentary evidence, saying, after a moment's inspection, "You're all right, sir; I can win this case for you." "Oh! you're a lawyer, then?" "Yes; when does your case come on?" "In an hour from now." "Well, now listen to me," said the Judge; "you go to the Court at that time, and ask the Court to continue the case until three o'clock this afternoon, as your counsel is unavoidably detained until then. Do you understand?" "All right. I'll do it, and come back to you." In due time the client returned with a favorable report. At three o'clock P. M., the Judge was in Court with his client, and won the case without delay. "What's your fee?" inquired the successful litigant, as they adjourned to take a drink. "One hundred dollars!" replied the Judge. The money was cheerfully paid, and the Judge pocketed his first fee in California. "I beg your pardon," said a man, confronting the Judge, as he turned from the bar, after their congratulatory imbibation, "I was in Court just now when you won that case, and I've got a little suit in the same Court. If you can put it through in the style you did our friend's case this afternoon, you're just the lawyer for my money." They sat down together, and after hearing the new client's case, the Judge took it in charge; was retained to be in Court at ten o'clock next morning, and repairing immediately to his late employer, resigned the position of *chef*, rented an office, and has since that day confined himself to the practice or the administration of law.

Geo. ———— tried his hand at street work in 1849, on Clay street, not as contractor, but in the shovel and pick interest; but one day's labor and one ounce in gold, as remuneration, was *quant. suff.* for George, who has since that day found more congenial employment as conveyancer, notary, broker, etc. We will tell why he came to leave street-work so abruptly, as an illustration of the quick transitions in San Francisco life in the spring of '50. As he was digging away, earning his "ounce," two men met close by and commenced conversation, but could not fully understand each other, as one spoke nothing but English, while the other was a Frenchman, comprehending only a few words of English. George, seeing the situation, very kindly explained the Frenchman's meaning. "What do you know about it?" abruptly inquired one of them—we needn't say it was not the citizen of the most courteous of nations. "Simply that I am a French scholar," said George. "Oh, ho!" answered the brusque individual. "What the d——l are you digging there for?" "One ounce a day," said our hero. "Then come out of it. I want you to make translations for me, on better pay." The bargain was made instanter, and George closed his street-grading interest that same evening, and commenced work on translations the next morning. This transition led to a connection and clientage among our French citizens, which our friend has retained until the present day.

One of the largest commission houses in San Francisco became bankrupt in a singular way—what might be termed retributive justice—the romance of commerce.

The firm had nearly all the English commission business in San Francisco, and among their account-current charges always put "Insurance ten per cent.," which was a myth—not the ten per cent!—that was solid coin in the firm's coffers—but the "insurance" on shipments—they never had a dollar insurance! One morning the fire swept everything, and the shippers said, "Pay us the insurance on our lost goods!" and the house was obliged to pay. It not only broke the firm, pecuniarily, but broke their hearts; they never rallied.

CHAPTER XIX.

George Hyde, Esq., the second Alcalde of San Francisco, arrived at Monterey on the U.S. frigate *Congress*, as Commodore Stockton's private secretary, on the 15th of July, 1846, and has been a resident of this State ever since that day. Judge Hyde is a Philadelphian; a gentleman of studious habits, refined tastes, and very reticent manners. No man who has ever occupied such a prominent place in San Francisco is less known by the public of to-day. The "Annals of San Francisco" makes no honorable mention of his name; but "thereby hangs a tale." In the spring of '50, Alcalde Hyde's office was on Clay street, near the Plaza. In the early days of '48 and '49 the Judge resided on Clay street, near Dupont, occupying the house since known as the "Sazerac," and kept by Mr. Samuel Gardner. After that time the Judge resided on Broadway, from whence he removed to the grassy lot near the junction of Post, Market and Montgomery streets, an enclosure of considerable size, half garden, half lawn; the house, a large, square, old-fashioned wooden building, considered quite out of town until '53–'54. Barry Hyde, the Judge's only son, is Alcalde of a Lower California *pueblo* at the present time.

Peter Toft arrived in California on the U. S. ship *Ohio*, Commodore Ap. Catesby Jones. Toft shipped as a common sailor, with a very slight knowledge of the English language, although a master of Greek, Latin and several modern languages. Toft's deportment and studious habits attracted the attention of Commodore Jones, who allowed him books from the library, and Toft was nearly a master of English on his arrival in California. His experience has been varied in our State: a miner, a painter, draughtsman, writer for newspapers, magazines, theatres, etc.; a traveler and naturalist; ever industrious, obliging and amiable; by birth a Dane, by adoption an American citizen. Mr. Toft has been in London for the last two or three years, engaged in painting and literary pursuits, but we hope for his return to San Francisco during this year.

James Nelson was agent for the pilots in '50, and was engaged in lightering ships and coaling steamboats for Charles Minturn. Mr. Nelson lived on board the storeship *Resoluta*, which used to lay off Cunningham's Wharf. Mr. Nelson was a very liberal, kind man, and assisted many to good fortune. B. M. Hartshorne was a partner of Mr. Nelson, and also lived on board the *Resoluta*. For a score of years Mr. Hartshorne has endeavored to make everybody believe that he is an unamiable, gruff, taciturn, morose individual; but his brusque manner has availed him nothing. We know his kind heart and his many charitable deeds. He is a hypocrite turned inside out—one of the best of men; ever shunning thanks and gratitude. Mr. Hartshorne was for many years president of the Cal. Steam Navigation Co.

J. & M. Phelan were wholesale liquor-dealers on Jackson street, north side, on the spot where so many circus troupes have shown in years gone by. The store then occupied by the Phelan brothers was a very large wooden structure, just such as we see now-a-days erected to protect stone-dressers engaged in the work for some public building—a big shed, with doors. Being down in a hollow, it was found necessary, after a heavy rain, to lay planks upon supports, to enable the visitor to reach the store dryshod;

and inside, similar means were used to get around among the stacks of casks and packages composing the firm's stock in trade, which was always large and valuable, the firm being one of the most successful in that line of business in San Francisco. J. Phelan is still living, but his brother died many years ago.

Bingham, Reynolds & Bartlett were on the corner of Broadway and Sansome, in a three or four story wooden building, we forget which; but in our memory the store was a tall, dusty-brown building. They did a thriving business in the spring of '50. Messrs. Bingham and Bartlett are both dead. Of Mr. Reynolds we do not know. Mr. Bingham was for many years, subsequent to the dissolution of the firm, in the City Clerk's office, in the City Hall, which post he occupied until his death. He was a faithful officer and a good man.

Mr. McShane, the manager of the Occidental Hotel for the last few years, was with W. T. Coleman & Co., in the same block with Bingham, Reynolds & Bartlett. Mr. Beideman, of "Beideman's Tract," used to be often in this neighborhood. He and John Piper were interested, either in business or outside lands, with

Samuel Fleishhacker, who, after the fire of May, '51, occupied a store on Pacific street, next to the southeast corner of Pacific and Sansome.

Tim. Burnham, formerly purser's clerk in the U. S. Navy, had a butcher's shop on the north side of Pacific wharf, near the store-ship *Arkansas*. Mr. Burnham was an accomplished amateur vocalist, and with Jas. Gamble and Charley Yeomans, used to sing in the choir of the Rev. Albert Williams' church. They made no pretensions as vocalists, but their voices harmonized perfectly, and, singing so frequently together, produced the most charming effect. Mr. Burnham returned to his old profession in the U. S. navy, died, and was buried at sea. Mr. Yeomans was for many years since then on the Petaluma steamer. We think that Mr. Gamble is in business in Newark, N. J. Even the memory of this trio's harmony is delightful. Chance brings together such voices—three of the greatest singers in the world might as vainly essay such harmony, as an ordinary voice to sing like the divine Parepa. The "Amphion Quartette" of to-day are the best harmonized male voices in the city, since Burnham, Gamble and Yeomans sang together.

O. Livermore was a rosy-cheeked boy, in the store of Wm. T. Coleman & Co., twenty-two or twenty-three years ago. Ready, willing, quick and good-natured, he became a favorite with his employers, and the up-river merchants trading with them, who were not few in those days. He rose to a position of trust and importance. For many years after leaving W. T. C. & Co's house, he was in the employ of Pioche, Bayerque & Co., in a very confidential position. His strict business integrity has placed him in charge of valuable estates, seldom entrusted to so young an agent. We sincerely hope that twenty-three years hence may find him as hale and useful as to-day.

In the same block with W. T. Coleman & Co's store, nearer to Pacific street, on the west side of Sansome, was the store of DeWitt & Harrison, one of the oldest firms in San Francisco established prior to the gold discovery. Alfred DeWitt and Henry A. Harrison were the members of the firm at that time. Since then the house has conducted business under the firm name of DeWitt, Kittle & Co., and now as Kittle & Co.

Mr. Kittle was a clerk for DeWitt & Harrison in 1850. W. T. Hoffman and young Twiggs—we forget his given name, he was always called

General Twiggs—were clerks in the same house. Case, Heiser & Co. and Florence Mahoney were in business in this same block. All of them are long since dead, and nothing but good is remembered of them. Ripley & McCullough were on the Pacific street corner of the same block, and were agents for the sale of the famous McCullough Shot. Mr. Ripley was killed by the explosion on board the *Jenny Lind;* and his wife and little daughter, who had just arrived in California, perished with him. Mr. McCullough has since been a banker in Virginia City, Nevada, for many years. Wm. M. Tileston had a portion of Ripley & McCullough's store, in May, 1851. Mr. Tileston was a brother of Tileston, of the firm of Spofford & Tileston, New York City.

Henry Mellen was a boy in W. T. Coleman & Co's store on Sansome street, and grew to manhood in their employ, serving them long and faithfully. He left the house to join the army, where he served his country with the same fidelity which distinguished his mercantile career. He is now a retired officer, having lost both of his feet in the service of his country.

Dore & Ross were on Sansome street, next to the southeast corner of Pacific, in May, '51, as importers and dealers in brandies and wines. Mr. Ross died many years since. He was a kind, honest, noble-hearted Irishman. Maurice Dore, of the old firm, is now the most prominent real-estate operator in San Francisco. Barry & Patten were on the southeast corner of Sansome and Pacific.

The conflagration of Sunday morning, June 22d, 1851, was stopped at this corner by nailing blankets on the front of the building, and keeping them saturated with water. Dewitt & Harrison's store, on the west side of Sansome, north of Pacific, was saved by blankets, on which was poured 80,000 gallons of vinegar.

A little way around the corner of Sansome, on Broadway, towards Battery street, was the grocery of Wm. H. Towne. We have never seen or heard of him since the summer of '50, having no occasion to be in that vicinity, subsequent to one day in June, when we were in his store awhile. But we remember him as being so very unlike the majority of bustling, excited, noisy and abrupt storekeepers of that strange, golden time—a pale, quiet man, with a soft voice, and a smile sweet as a woman's; a man suggesting the painter, the poet, the musician; with thoughts like Schubert's—anything but a grocer. We remember the peculiarity of his complexion; golden-red hair, singularly black eyes, and a delicate, pale face. We did not occupy ten minutes in our business conversation, and have never met since that day in June, twenty-three years ago; but his face is retained in our memory, curiously vivid, and oftentimes returning through all these years—an unaccountable mnemonic vagary.

Towards noon, on the day of the fire, after the flames were well subdued, a sailor lad from a French ship in the harbor was going up the hill on Pacific street, half way between Sansome and Montgomery, looking at the destruction on either side, when the idea occurred to him to light his pipe. Stooping down, he was endeavoring to scoop up a little burning coal with the bowl of his pipe, when some one of a crowd, passing at the moment, cried "Incendiary! incendiary!" With one impulse the men rushed at him, knocked him down, and almost instantly kicked the poor, innocent lad to death, and walked away, leaving the lifeless body lying in the street, mutilated past recognition. A moment before he had passed up the wharf in the health and hope of youth, his sunburnt cheek, bright eye and waving hair giving full promise of longevity. Walking on with childish curiosity—his first footsteps in a strange land—such a little way, ending in dreadful death.

The men who committed the terrible deed passed on, perhaps not realizing he was dead—not caring. They thought him an incendiary, worthy of death, and acted out the exasperation which filled the hearts of men suffering from repeated conflagrations.

No inquiry was made, for it was useless, and the tragic incident, with its victim, was soon forgotten; but it was a sickening illustration of the fact that chance is sometimes so dreadfully potent.

CHAPTER XX.

The clerks of a banking-house on Montgomery street, in the days when pans of gold-dust were standing on every counter in the business houses, had been greatly troubled with the gold-dust account. It would not balance — varying from thirty to sixty dollars every day. Every care was taken with it, but to no avail. Ben Smith, who had puzzled in vain over the books, concluded to look outside of them for a solution. For three successive days he weighed the dust with his own hands, placed it in the accustomed spot, and sat down in a hiding-place to watch. Every morning, soon after the trap was laid, a highly respectable man, a particular friend of the head of the house, came in, as usual, stood about awhile, passed the usual greetings, sauntered up to the pan, as was his habit for months, carefully examined the contents, rubbed it in his hands, dropped it out into the pan with a flourish, slapped his hands together, and walked to the door, stood for a moment, and then passed out. Soon as he had gone, Ben reweighed the dust, and found it several ounces short. This programme was repeated by both actors in the little comedy for three successive days. Perfectly satisfied, the clerk communicated with the banker. "Oh, there must be some mistake—some misapprehension—or perhaps a joke on one of his old friends," was the banker's exclamation. "The joke is a queer one to carry on so long," said Benjamin, proposing that the head of the house should take the "look-out's" chair, and watch the game himself. Reluctantly, he consented to spy upon his friend, and was convinced after watching two or three days, and seeing the gold-dust weighed immediately after his old friend's manipulation and departure. After this, he was forced to admit, much to every employee's relief, that the mystery was solved. The deficit for all the past months was promptly paid by the gentlemanly kleptomaniac, whose curiosity upon the subject of *oro en polvo*, as far as that particular bank was concerned, ceased from that moment.

Leonard Rowell, assistant superintendent of Wells, Fargo & Co's Express Department in San Francisco, arrived in San Francisco on the first of September, 1849, on the barque *Drummond*. Mr. Rowell, with Will Gay, a fellow passenger, landed at the corner of Central Wharf (now Commercial street) and Leidesdorff street, inquiring of the first person they met for the store of Lovering & Gay, Mr. Gay of that firm being a brother of Mr. Rowell's fellow-passenger. They soon found the store, which was on Montgomery street, just north of Central Wharf, and before they had been ten minutes in conversation, Mr. G. H. Howard came in and remarked to Mr. Charles Gay, that he wished a clerk to take account of the lumber about to be discharged from the brig *Belfast*, then lying in the stream. Mr. Gay turned to Mr. Rowell, and asked if he cared for the opportunity, when it was accepted at once most cheerfully, and Mr. Rowell commenced his business career in California within a half hour after his arrival, has continued it up to the present time, and is still employed. After the brig *Belfast* operation, at wages which nearly took his breath away, and board thrown in on the brig, *tambien*, he found employment of various kinds until he entered the office of Gregory's Express Co., then Adams & Co's Express; then in the office of the company where he now is, and where he has so long and competently discharged his various official duties.

The postage box in ———— & Co's express-office *was never balanced*. It couldn't be done. No one ever attempted it, because no one knew how to do it. It was the custom for clerk, messenger or driver, who wished to lunch, or "wet his whistle," to dip in the postage box. There was nothing secret or sly about it; it was customary, and no one thought it anything out of the ordinary course, and we merely mention it to illustrate the liberality and looseness of those days. In the Sacramento office of the company the same custom prevailed.

One morning Charley King, the well known actor, came in and asked for Billy L————, one of the clerks in the office, noted for his extensive wardrobe, and an ambition to rival Dick Stanly in fashionable attire. "Where is Billy?" inquired King. "He is out just at this moment—anything that we can do for you?" replied one of the accommodating clerks—and, by the way, the clerks in the express and banking houses *were* accommodating in those days. "I want to pay Billy L———— ten dollars which I borrowed from him last night," said King, taking an eagle from his pocket, and standing with it between his fingers, as if he wished some one to say they would give it to his friend L————. "I think he'll be in if you'll wait a moment," said somebody. King seemed in haste, when "Blaize," who was behind the counter, said, with that irresistible humor of tone, peculiarly his own: "Oh, put it in the 'postage-box,' Charley! He'll find it there!"

The express companies numbered six in early days. Adams & Co's express to "The United States" advertised to forward gold-dust and packages by every steamer. Their office was on Montgomery street, between California and Sacramento.

Berford & Co's express, on Clay street—Plaza—advertised to forward packages to San José every day, Sunday excepted.

Gregory's express—office on Jackson street wharf—advertised to forward gold-dust and packages to all parts of the world by every steamer; also to Sacramento and the northern mines daily.

Haven & Co's express—office on Montgomery street, where the London and Liverpool and Globe Insurance Co's office since stood—also advertised to do the same.

Hawley & Co's express office was on Montgomery, between Sacramento and California. They carried only to the interior California towns.

Todd & Co's express, in the same block, carried to Stockton and the southern mines only.

The business of ——— & Co's express office was so great—its ramifications so extended—that its president and directors were desirous to know its profits, its expenses and condition. Its chief and founder came out to ascertain. On the California steamer from New York, he was the recipient of such assiduous and obsequious attention as might be offered to the President of the United States upon his travels. On the Panama railroad and on the Pacific steamers it was the same—one continued ovation until he reached the wharf in San Francisco. Here the reception of the company's agents in California was so affectionate and overwhelming, that the worthy president, modest by nature, was helpless to resist the thought that he was at the head of a mighty power in the land. A gay barouche, drawn by four high-stepping steeds, awaited him, and, like a great conqueror making his triumphal entry, he rode to apartments worthy of a king. The dinner that awaited him opened wide his honest, practical, old business eyes. The *chef's* artistic delicacies in such profusion, the many and choice wines, the table equipage, and the attendants, bewildered the unassuming and industrious head of the company. A business warranting such luxury and splendor was far above his wildest flight of fancy.

One or two gentle expressions of surprise at the surroundings were received with the look of men not quite comprehending, or, perhaps, rather surprised at their honored guest's remark upon an every-day matter, but too well bred to notice it. After an elaborate dessert, the guest hinted his wish to retire early, that he might be prepared for business in the morning, and was escorted to rest by his solicitous and hospitable hosts.

Early the next morning—long before the agents or clerks came to their posts—the worthy president, neat, smooth-shaved, and dressed becoming a business man, was pacing impatiently up and down the outer office. When the San Francisco managers appeared, they smilingly said, in answer to his proposition that they should proceed to business: "Not to-day! Oh, no, sir; not to-day! You require rest; we can't allow you to fatigue yourself just off this long, tedious trip!"

It was useless to remonstrate—to protest that the whole journey had been one long rest; that he never felt better in his life, and was perfectly ready for business; that his time was limited, and he must be expeditious. He was told in the most blandly courteous manner, that he must not forget that he never could, with impunity, exert or fatigue himself *in this climate* as at home; that the statements were preparing, and would be ready in a few days; but to-day a party had been made up to visit a certain place, in honor of himself, and they were about ready to start. What could he do? Nothing but acquiesce, then, and he went with his entertainers; but he resolved to go on no more pleasure parties until business was settled. His resolutions were of no avail.

New excursions, wonderful sights, great natural curiosities, must be visited; it would never do to return without having looked upon these world-wide wonders; expressed desires, remonstrances, expostulations, all were smiled away; they hurried him from place to place, in one continued whirl, received here and passed on there, with honors and attentions never ending. His methodical life up to this time was so broken in upon, his systematic habits so diverted, that his health was disturbed, and, like a prudent general, convinced of the futility of farther fighting, he wisely beat a retreat. His proposition to send out a trusty, plodding, old, confidential clerk to arrange the business *which his delightful round of continued pleasure and ever increasing knowledge of the country's wonderful resources had caused him to neglect*, was the only way by which he could cover his retreat with self-respect, and cheat himself into the belief that his crafty agents had not outwitted him. Soon as it was possible, after his return to his home on the Atlantic side, there came out to San Francisco a tall, grave, white-haired man, sedate and venerable, with full authority, etc. The agents and the old, confidential, white-haired emissary crossed their swords warily, fencing and parrying with utmost caution, until accident revealed, through a chink in the old man's armor, his weak spot—Schnapps. The crafty fencer touched with his keen rapier the vulnerable point; off fell the disguising armor, and the jolliest old man conceivable stood revealed. The hospitable hosts gave unremitting attention. They whirled him faster than they had ever whirled his worthy chief. The old man laughed so incessantly that he could not give his mind to dry business details. He laughingly proposed to leave for home, rode to the steamer, laughing, and laughed more than ever when he found his state-room lined with cases of his favorite schnapps, and sailed away still laughing. The managers laughed—within their sleeves—when he had gone, and held high carnival. But soon the inevitable crash came, and the insiders, heads of the house and clerks, laughed in their sleeves immoderately; but the poor outsiders, save the bench and bar, felt like doing anything but laughing.

CHAPTER XXI.

Captain Charles L. Wiggin arrived in San Francisco on the schooner *Eudorus*, September 14th, 1849. The store subsequently occupied by C. C. Richmond, on Jackson, near the corner of Montgomery, was part of the freight on board the *Eudorus*.

Captain Wiggin first stepped on shore where Montgomery now crosses Jackson. Then it was a sea beach, the tide sometimes coming as high as the present northwest corner of Montgomery and Jackson. Captain W. was the first officer of the steamer *Midas*, when she doubled the Cape of Good Hope, and subsequently was her commander.

The *Midas* was the first American steamer that ever doubled Good Hope or Cape Horn. She was a small propeller, built by Ericsson, and owned by R. B. Forbes, in whose employ the subject of our sketch sailed, from 1835 to 1849. Captain Wiggin was a boy on board one of Mr. Forbes' ships, in the harbor of Hong

Kong, when the site of that now populous city was occupied only by bamboo huts.

The ship *Oxnard*, Captain Cole, arrived in San Francisco, November 22d, 1849, bringing twenty-five wooden houses, all numbered in sections, and fitted in Boston, for erection in San Francisco. Charles R. Bond brought them out for Wm. D. M. Howard, who retained twelve of them, after selling twelve to Captain J. L. Folsom, and one to Captain Cole.

Three or four of them were erected on Mission street, near Third, Messrs. Howard, Mellus and Brannan occupying three of them. Captain Folsom erected others on Mission, between First and Second streets; on Minna, Natoma, Tehama and Folsom streets. To Mrs. Van Winkle, Mrs. Cany and Mrs. Wakeman, whose husbands were all attached to his office, Captain Folsom gave each a cottage, and, we believe, nearly all of the buildings stand to-day. The house in which Mr. Howard resided, prior to the *Oxnard's* arrival, was on the northeast corner of Washington and Stockton streets. Some years ago it was moved to Bryant street, between Second and Third, where it stands at the present writing.

It is a fact worthy of record, that none of

these houses brought out on the *Oxnard* were ever burned. The first Orphan Asylum in San Francisco was opened in one of these houses, on the corner of Folsom and Second streets, on General Halleck's land.

The house was contributed by Mr. Howard. The managers of the Asylum were Mrs. S. R. Throckmorton, Mrs. C. V. Gillespie, and, we believe, Mrs. Henry Haight and Mrs. R. J. Vandewater. We are quite certain that some of these ladies have, through all the years since the little wooden cottage was given as a home to the fatherless, worked zealously for those "little ones." May the God of the widow and the fatherless bless them, and the memory of the late Abner Barker, who left twenty-five thousand dollars to that noble charity.

Wm. D. M. Howard's office, at the time of the fire of June 14, 1850, was on the southeast corner of Leidesdorff and Long Wharf (now Commercial street), and in the same building with the P. M. S. S. Co's office.

There was a high gate across the head of the wharf, from the corner of this building. Subsequent to the fire, Mr. Howard took the old adobe kitchen of the Hudson Bay Co's house, roofed it, and made it suitable for an office, until the erection of the brick building so long occupied in the lower story by Wm. H. Keith, apothecary.

At the old office, in the adobe kitchen, and in the new one, and about its entrance, the old pioneers used to congregate. They were genial, hospitable men, with scarcely any exception; men whose word bound them entirely and sacredly. In 1849 a roundabout blue jacket and black pants in cool weather; in warm days, white was the costume. Even into 1850, some wore the old California style of dress. Mr. Vioget always did, and we believe we have seen others wearing the old style Californian costume as late as the summer of 1850; but the fashions prevailing among the people drawn to San Francisco by the gold discovery, were adopted by all at last, save Mr. Vioget, whom we never saw dressed in them.

In the delicious January days of California, when the warm sun kisses the earth into new life and smiling brightness, and nature seems kinder to mankind than elsewhere, we always recall just such a time, when we saw a group of the early pioneers standing before the office of Wm. D. M. Howard, the kindest and noblest of them all. There was Captain Cooper, Jacob P. Leese, Mr. Vioget, Thomas O. Larkin, Henry

Teschemacher, Alfred Robinson, Don Juan Foster, Don Abel Stearns, Dr. Denn, Don Juan Thompson, —— Richardson, Robert A. Parker and several others.

Henry Teschemacher was then, always has been, and is to-day, the soul of honor, courage and modesty; perfectly unassuming, proverbially courteous, extremely reticent as to himself, but never to be moved an inch, or ignored for an instant, when acting for his friends. In 184– a difficulty occurred between Lieut. Bonnycastle and Henry Mellus. Mr. Mellus received a challenge; but Mr. Teschemacher insisted upon assuming the responsibility of the affair, upon the grounds that Mr. Mellus, being just married, ought not to jeopard his life, and could not be so well spared as his bachelor friend.

Mr. Teschemacher and Lieut. Bonnycastle fought with rifles; the former escaping unhurt, shooting off a finger from the hand of his antagonist. Mr. Teschemacher won the choice of weapons, and selected his antagonist's favorite rifle; otherwise the result might have been different. Mr. Teschemacher never sought office; but the citizens of San Francisco thrice elected him to the office of Mayor by a most flattering majority, notwithstanding his earnest efforts to escape the honor.

William D. M. Howard was a man to draw other men around him, not by self-assertion, by promises, or studied, conventional courteousness, but by the magnetism of his genuine, heartfelt cordiality. His fellow men intuitively recognized his nature, and liked to be with one of whom they felt so sure, in whom they fully trusted, without hesitation.

The native Californians ever found him a good adviser and true friend; and all who came to him, seeking their fortunes on these shores, were most generously befriended. If "he who giveth to the poor, lendeth to the Lord," Mr. Howard resigned earthly wealth for far greater treasure in Heaven.

Not all the pioneers were men of honor. There are exceptions to prove every rule, although it seems odd to find its application among the men who came to California as real pioneers, before the excited rush for gold. People of later days ask, "How is it that the old pioneers were such exceptional men? Was it not the fact that they were like any other men, only, being few in numbers and living under similar circumstances, peculiarly peaceful and contented, the strifes and contentions of politics and litigation were unknown, and their undisturbed friendship, so long continued, is now, in memory, surrounded by a halo, placing them apart from other men?" To which we reply, that undoubtedly those very circumstances strongly cemented the ties then formed; yet they were men, by nature, of broader minds, and possessed of a foresight unusual in most men, freer in thought and habit—the very attributes belonging to pioneers, through which Nature herself set them apart from other men, constituting them the vanguard of the long, trans-continental march of emigration's endless army.

In 1847, J. J. Vioget made the first survey of San Francisco, or Yerba Buena, and laid out the plan for its streets. Had his design been carried into effect, it would, as a sanitary proposition, have been much better for the city's inhabitants. Every house would have had an equal share of the sun upon its front and rear during the day. Political scheming, that bane of republics, changed the plan to give one of its party favorites a *job*, causing, in this particular instance, injury to the health of thousands. Vioget's wisdom and experience sought to obviate and prevent this harmful condition of things, for he knew the value of the sun's light and heat in San Francisco, where he had lived much of the time since 1837, and noted the isothermal needs. M. Vioget was Swiss, of French descent, like the great Agassiz, who, when speaking, always reminds us of Vioget, so modest, earnest and fascinating in conversation, always imparting some new and useful knowledge; eager as a child to gain a scrap of information; and, withal, a wonderful way of drawing from you, by no effort of your own, better things than you imagined yourself capable of saying—the most intoxicating of all flatteries. Vioget resided on Kearny street, west side, adjoining the old City Hotel, which formed the southwest corner of Clay and Kearny. In stature he was about five feet eight and a half inches, and possessed of a good average avoirdupois. He carried his head a little inclined, like one listening; his hair was short, plentiful and very gray; he wore a full, gray "old guard" moustache; and up to the last day that we saw him, he wore the old Californian costume—the short blue jacket and black pants. Few, to-day, save the old residents, seem to remember him, so reticent was his nature. We do not even find his name in Kimball's San Francisco Directory of 1850. But we should be happy to think that these pages might be the means of reminding the victims of malarious ills, of rheumatism, and chills and fever, that the subject of this sketch labored for their good a quarter of a century ago, though thwarted by that hydra—politics.

CHAPTER XXII.

There was a real, old English strolling pan-pipe player in San Francisco during the days of which we write—a fellow who reminded us of the summer afternoon when Little Nell and the old man came upon Short and Codlin, sitting among the grave-stones of the old church-yard, repairing their *fautoccini*. Our pioneer pan-piper (we believe he was eligible to the association), played upon the cymbals, triangle, accordeon and bass-drum—a genuine itinerant of the "Merrie Englande" fair and race grounds. He came from Sydney to this city, and was a character—a study. He wore the narrow-brimmed, very high-crowned hat, found only upon the heads of H. B. M. subjects—just the pattern in everything, save color, of the pioneer candy man's (also eligible) hat, on Montgomery street, —his hat being a rusty black, the pan-piper's a light brown. His shirt-collar and cravat were very elaborate, and the fashion of his coat and nether garments dignified and recondite. The expression of his face, as he jerked his head right and left, in the execution of an *allegro vivace* movement, with octave intervals, was truly indescribable. As his mouth traveled along the edge of the pipes, the action of the *levator labii proprius* and risible muscles, gave a hearty, enjoyable grin along the facial angle, contrasting ludicrously with the lachrymose appearance of his eyes, from the elevation of the inner extremity of the eyebrows, the sensitive movement of the *occipito frontalis*, and the despondent droop of the eyelid, like one who had blown upon dying embers until the dizzy brain ached with the exertion. His face recalled Pliny's words:

"Frons hominis tristitiæ, hilaritatis, clementiæ, severitatis, index est."

One could not repress a smile, on giving him the most casual glance; but to stop one's ears, and watch his appearance for a moment, taking in its mingled absurdity and serious work-a-day earnestness, through the single sense of sight, was enough to convulse with laughter the most lugubrious of men. This disciple of the shepherd's deity worked hard upon his pipes and drum, earning well the harvest that he gathered. Some time in the early part of '52 he disappeared—we suppose went to Australia, or some secluded village in old England, where he dreams away the evening of his life, discarding pipe of Pan for pipe nicotian. We can never forget him, nor the amusement he afforded us, being at that time fresh from the study of "The Anatomy and Philosophy of Expression, as connected with the fine arts," by Sir Charles Bell, K. H.

One of our San Francisco aristocracy was formerly a crockery and earthenware dealer, on the Atlantic side of the continent, but did not pursue his old trade in California, making more money in various ways, from hotel keeping to real estate speculating, etc. After accumulating a fortune, he, of course, followed the old, stereotyped path—went to some other country to spend it. Meeting a congenial spirit in Europe, they traveled the grand tour together, each playing the *rentier*, the *grand proprietaire*, entirely ignoring any knowledge of business, of any nature whatsoever. They were together in Paris, on the Rhine, in Dresden, Berlin, Vienna, Venice, Florence, Rome, and finally came to Herculaneum and Pompeii, where they were lost in the wonders of the long buried past.

One day, as they were examining some curious specimens of ancient pottery—bowls, cups, dishes and recondite platters, in one of the unearthed palaces of Pompeii, our California *rentier* became genuinely interested in a singularly delicate thin bowl of very hard, bell-like material, that vibrated with a gentle ring in handling. Turning it carefully over, he scrutinized it inwardly, outwardly and at its edge; held it up to the light, with every look and movement denoting the expert, but all unconscious of the watchful eyes of his companion. Suddenly, after a long inspection, he tossed the bowl with his right hand, caught it on the extended finger-tips of his left, held it in silent poise, like a prestidigitateur, giving it a quick tap with the middle finger knuckle of the other hand. At the clear bell-like ring, his face glowed with the undisguised satisfaction of an approving virtuoso in Chinaware and crockery. "No! you don't say so? I used to be in that line too." "Eh, what did you say?" asked the California *rentier*, suddenly roused from his preoccupation, and turning a dismayed face to his companion. "What line? Don't understand you!" "Oh, bosh!" said the other, "I have been too many years in the business not to know you by the way you handled that bowl just now. We'll understand each other all the better now." "I don't understand you at all, sir," said the silly Californian, whose vanity was so wounded that he actually turned his back upon his good-natured companion, and never resumed the acquaintance.

There was a Mr. Baker—we believe his name was William Baker—who, we think, was one of the firm of S. H. Williams & Co., or a clerk in that house in the spring of '50. We remember Mr. Baker as being the most carefully and neatly dressed man in San Francisco at that time; not that there were not other men as well dressed in material, as neat and punctiliously clean, but people, as a general thing in those days, wore gray or brown, or blue, or drab, and spotted or striped shirts of fancy colors. This Mr. Baker always wore a full suit of black, and spotless linen; his hat, only, was an approach to color, being a soft, broad-brimmed, low, round-crowned beaver, of a brownish, raw umber shade. We used to marvel at Mr. Baker's invariably neat, spotless attire, and wonder how he preserved his wardrobe, amid the never-ceasing clouds of dust that were ever floating in the air through our unpaved streets. He never seemed in the least ruffled or annoyed by the trampling mule teams and their following clouds. He walked along as if on the clean swept walks of Philadelphia, Boston, or the

Boulevards of Paris, his faultless shirt and collar, his ample wristbands, his Poole-like coat, vest and pants, his patent-leather boots, facing the flying, powdery nuisance more bravely than any flannel shirt and duck trousers in the whole town. His utter obliviousness to dust, and his unvarying suit of new black broadcloth, was ever a mystery to us, and we believed in the spring of '50, and still believe, that he had three hundred and sixty-five new black suits, with linen and patent-leathers to match.

Malachi Fallon was City Marshal in the spring of '50. He was a good officer and an honest man. In '51 Mr. Fallon opened the Rip Van Winkle House, on the corner of Pacific Wharf and Battery street. Subsequently he purchased of Messrs. E. V. Joice and Daniel Lockwood the Knickerbocker House, on the corner of Long Wharf and Battery street. Mr. Fallon is at the present time living in Oakland, and is to all appearance in health and vigor. We hope he may live and enjoy another score of years. When Wells, Fargo & Co. opened in '52 at 114 Montgomery street, next door south of Barry & Patten's, Mr. Joseph Fallon (brother of Malachi), John Bell and Mr. Birdsall were the only employees of that express company. The office is still next door to Barry & Patten's, but on the opposite side of the street. John Bell and Birdsall are still in the office, and Mr. Fallon, we believe, is in Honolulu.

Mr. Daniel Lockwood died in Newark, N. J., several years since.

Mr. Joice, is and has been for many years, a notary, and bids fair to live a half century longer, if one may judge by his step and manner on California street; and better still, by the ground he will get over, and the steep hillsides he can climb, in a day's shooting, coming in full of spirit and fun, when some of the boys are lame and disagreeably quiet. We hope he may bag his game for many years to come, for we do certainly like good-natured men.

Swift & Brother, James and S. C. Swift, were general merchants on Sacramento street, between Montgomery and Kearny, in the spring of '50. John B. Bourne, a brother-in-law of one of the firm, was employed with them. The fire of June 14th, '50, burned them out. Mr. Bourne went on a voyage of speculation to Callao in the following October, returned in the spring of '51, and rented one of a block of stores on Long Wharf, adjoining the storeship *Apollo*. Mr. Bourne hired this store of Mr. Chase, a carpenter, who built and owned the block.

Saturday evening Mr. Chase called in for his rent—rents were payable in advance—which Mr. Bourne paid—$1400 per month. This was about sunset, and before midnight his store, as well as his rent money, had disappeared. Mr. Bourne seems just as well able to-day to bear misfortune as he was twenty years ago.

John A. McGlynn was City Recorder, and his office was in the City Hall in '50. Dan. C. McGlynn was a dealer in paints and oils on Sacramento street, near Montgomery. Their homes and their interests have been with us ever since that time, and they are worthy citizens.

Balley & Hooper were merchants on the corner of Montgomery and Pacific in 1850. We think Mr. Balley was afterwards of the firm of Edwards, Balley & Co. Mr. B. was an unselfish, benevolent man, and lost his life by an act of courtesy to a lady, who was one of a party coming down the Sacramento river to San Francisco. When the steamer came to the bay, the sudden change of atmosphere caused the lady to express her fear of taking cold, if she remained on deck. Mr. Balley immediately removed his cloak and wrapped it about the form of his fair companion, but this act of gallantry cost him his life, as he then contracted a cold from which he never recovered.

John H. Saunders arrived in San Francisco on the twentieth of June, 1850, on the steamer *Tennessee*. S. R. Throckmorton, Lieut. Beale (subsequently Surveyor-General of California), Messrs. Berri and May (of Davidson & Co.), James L. King, Leonard Skinner, Chetwood & Edwards, and many others well known, were on the same steamer. Mr. Saunders has since been City Attorney for San Francisco, and State Senator from San Francisco. He is a virtuoso, a skillful amateur musician, and a generous, honorable man.

Thomas G. Cary was with Macondray & Co. in 1850, and subsequently was one of the firm. Mr. Cary was a merchant, a scholar, a student, an ichthyologist; an accomplished master in self-defense, a gentleman, and a rare good fellow. He left California about ten years since, and has been very busily occupied nearly all that time in the museum of zoölogy at Harvard College, Cambridge, Mass.

I. Friedlander was a busy man in San Francisco in 1850, and has been ever since. He is a Field Marshal in California's army of speculators—marshals his forces, and moves with mighty results. He has brains and sagacity, generosity, honor and gratitude, and never forgets a favor from high or low; but any unfairness toward Mr. Friedlander has not been found remunerative.

CHAPTER XXIII.

The road or track to the Presidio, twenty years ago, was not as comfortable for a drive as at the present day. No level way for vehicles along the hard, steep-sloping hill, corrugated with rain-washed ruts and ugly gulleys. It was a most uninviting ride for those in the saddle; but to drive in a vehicle across that old Presidio road, was neither safe nor pleasant. There were many ways of scaling the hill—we mean to say pathways to the hill—but the most traveled was the one off Powell street, near Washington Square. The hard adobe soil in summer was like stone, and in the rainy season gummy, sticky and disagreeable. The steep, shelving, uneven way, making the carriage perpetually seem as if it were just toppling over, or sliding down the precipitous hill, was very trying to the nerves of those penned in upon the back seat; and when we remember that old, uneven, rutted, gulley-worn road, we wonder how we ever had the courage to travel it in any way, other than in the saddle. Like all primitive roads, it wound up over the highest, most toilsome way, past cattle-pens and corrals, brick-yards and butcher's shambles, the ground all the way looking as baked and hard as slag or adamant, with no sign of vegetation, but everywhere a surface, seemingly blown bare by the continuous winds of summer. After the rains, 'twas difficult to believe in such a change. The tender emerald grass and dotting wild flowers, the soft, soothing air, winning us to forgetfulness of the harsh summer gales, parching the skin, fretting the eyes, and spoiling the hair and temper. In the dry, dusty season, it was pleasant to come upon the little grove of trees where Leonidas Haskell's house stood, and where he afterwards built three cottages, one of which was occupied by John C. Fremont. Trees were very grateful to the eyes of San Franciscans in those days, when homes and gardens and shrubbery were not yet planted, and hearts were not rooted to the country, entwined with the old associations and affections belonging with "home" in every clime.

When we had passed Mr. Haskell's house, we were descending the western slope of the hill, and turned southward a little way; then down again westwardly to the little lane, past the brick yard to the little grocery, making the corner of the block where the French gardeners cultivated their vegetables for the city markets. The Sutter street railroad uses this same road now for their Harbor View track. In those days, the road abruptly descended to a little hollow, which was impassable often in the rainy season, obliging the traveler to skirt the high bank on the north side, at the edge of the garden on the other side, kept by another citizen of *La Belle France*. Beyond this little hollow, was another very abrupt little rise, which brought you to the road leading to the "Laguna," or Washerwoman's Bay, where Ansel I. Easton's laundry was busy at work upon the P. M. S. S. Co's linen—a never-ending labor in those days of Panama travel. Mr. James Laidley has built a residence on this spot, and has changed the appearance of things beyond recognition. Farther on were cow-sheds and barns, and milk-ranches, a little wayside inn, where soldiers, with a day's liberty from the Presidio barracks, might come and enjoy lager and liberty combined. A few cottages were beside the road, at intervals, until the Government Reserve was reached, and the Presidio, which was then a few dilapidated, old adobes, some long, shed-like barracks, and a cottage or two for the officers' quarters—no more like the Presidio of to-day than the fort at Fort Point now is like the one built by the old Spaniards. Leaving out the question of utility, the old fort was far more picturesque and charming to visit than the red brick, angular, menacing pile of defense now usurping its place. We must confess to the belief that the old Spanish fort would have made a short and sorry fight, as compared with its mighty successor. Still, we shall always remember the old one, and our visits to it, with a pleasurable feeling, which never could be awakened by any amount of intimacy with the fort of to-day.

There was such an air of romance about the old, gray, crumbling walls and moldering ramparts; such a mute significance upon the face of everything within those silent walls, upon the cliff that overhung the foamy beach. The decaying gun-carriage, with wheels half buried in the weeds and grass; the rusty, old, iron ring we stooped to lift, and found it fast in the old plank scuttle; some hidden cell, or water-tank, provided for a siege. The weather-worn embrasures, that scores of years ago framed in the faces of seaward-gazing sentry, and *commandante*, grave and thoughtful—now, but the basking-place where sea-birds rest awhile, blinking in the warm sunlight, and gathering fresh strength, again sail out upon the winds, and scream above the sea, whose monotone beating its cadence on the rocky shore had, years ago, sung the old fort to everlasting rest.

This was the end of the Presidio road. Horsemen often went on over the hill beyond the fort to Point Lobos, and to the cliff, where now the Cliff House stands, and halted to watch the *platyrhynchus* of Cuvier, now popularly known as Captain Foster's sea lions. The man of to-day, lounging luxuriantly in a cane chair upon the broad, sheltering balcony, leisurely watching through a good glass the clumsy gambols of Captain Foster's stock, with the best of viands, wines and fragrant weeds at his command, has the advantage of him who, in the saddle or on foot, breasted the winds and dust over the heavy path, with its ending on the open cliff—shelterless and supperless. Some went on by the beach to the old Ocean House, and in to the Mission by the hill where the Industrial School now stands. Some by another way, between Lone Mountain and the other hills, where, near a little lake, stood a small wayside house, whose occupant dispensed milk-punch, refreshing, rich and cool. This way led to the Mission (nearer than by the beach) across the open, primitive and unfenced country, upon whose broad-spreading acres most of the thoughtless riders looked, as upon so much dirt; while a few, with sagacious foresight, seized the opportunity, making for themselves great fortunes.

The Russ family came to California on the ship *Loo Choo*, with Stevenson's Regiment, and were, altogether, we believe—father, mother, sons and daughters—twelve in number. The old house at the corner of Sixth and Harrison streets, on the block known as Russ' Garden, was standing a year or two since. J. C. C. & A. G. Russ, goldsmiths and jewelers, lived there in 1850, and had their store on Montgomery, between Pacific and Broadway.

Russ' Garden was a famous suburban resort twenty years ago for the German citizens' May-day festivities, Sunday-school picnics and miscellaneous merry-makings. The garden was a little, dry knoll in the middle of a swamp, and the rider who came along the narrow road built from Folsom street to the garden, mired his horse if he deviated in the least from the track. As late as '55, we have seen horses and cows swamped on both sides of the Folsom street plank-road, and on the east side of the road leading to the garden. To-day it would be difficult to see any traces of the old neighborhood; all seems alike south of Market street. The Russ family had a house on Bush street, just above where the Russ House stands. A large, three-story, wooden hotel used to occupy part of the ground on Montgomery street now covered by the Russ.

Mr. Otto Kloppenburg, formerly City Treasurer, kept a grocery store on the Russ House corner of Bush and Montgomery. Peyser Bros. kept a clothing store on this block for twenty years or more, and took the corner of Bush street when the Russ House was built. There they remained until within a few months, when they sold out their lease to Mr. Raphael, who carries on the same business. The Russ family have always been good citizens, and deserve the fortune which has come to them by the appreciation of the land they had the prudent foresight to secure and improve.

Gladwin & Whitmore were merchants on California street, between Montgomery and Sansome. Horace M. Whitmore, of this firm, was always an enthusiastic Californian, a firm believer in his adopted State's eventual permanence, commercially and agriculturally, in its climatic advantages, and their certain influence in its future population. It was through Mr.

Whitmore's persistent labors, with the invaluable aid of Professor Davidson, of the United States Coast Survey, that the Limantour Fraud was detected and thwarted. Others have claimed the credit of that exposure, but the merit belongs where we have placed it. Mr. Whitmore was the first to agitate the widening of Kearny street, and followed up the enterprise with that tenacious, patient industry of purpose in a good cause, which was ever the business of his life. Few men in San Francisco had made so much happiness for so many people, by genuine, unostentatious kindness and charity, as Horace M. Whitmore. In 1849, Mr. Whitmore purchased the house built by Rodman M. Price, on California street, below Dupont, where he lived until the time of his death, two years since. Mr. Whitmore never was away from the State after his arrival, in 1849. He left a large estate, in which is the block known as Trainor's Row, on Kearny, corner of Sutter street.

CHAPTER XXIV.

The three-story wooden house on Dupont street, just south of the Congregational Church, on the southwest corner of California and Dupont, and occupied so many years by Mr. Tallant, the banker, was bought from the cargo of a wrecked ship, by General Cazneau, in the spring of 1850. Mr. Joseph Capprise, of Baltimore, superintended its erection. This house was fitted and prepared for building in the East, and shipped for California.

On the fourth of July, '50, this house was gaily decorated with flags of all nations—a novel proceeding in San Francisco, exciting much attention. Among the floating bunting was the green banner and its golden harp, which gave rise to the rumor that it was the residence of the Irish Consul. The old house, which stood so many years high up on the embankment, is now lowered to the street level, and changed past recognition.

General Thomas N. Cazneau, Hon. H. H.

Byrne and Mr. Joseph Capprise came to California on the same ship. The General looks no older than on the day of his arrival; but his two companions are sleeping in the necropolis, for whose inhabitants the sea sings everlastingly a mournful threnody.

The house of which we have elsewhere spoken, as erected by Judge Burritt, on the northwest corner of Stockton and Sutter streets, in 1851, was made and fitted for building, and shipped in Boston for San Francisco. Its twin was erected in Benicia by General Frisbie, and is at present, we believe, occupied by Captain Walsh. We have a vindictive feeling for the rascal who tried a few months since to burn the old house in San Francisco, which has long been a pleasant sight to the citizen who knew only its comfortable, home-like, Elizabethan exterior through so many long years, that it had become like the kind face of an old acquaintance. But those who were more fortunate, and knew the welcome of its interior in Lucien Hermann's and Dr. Bowie's time, can never forget the genuine hospitality, nor the fascinating conversational power of their courteous hosts.

John S. Ellis had a shipping office in San Francisco, in 1850. We think the firm was Ellis

& Goin—Thomas Goin; and that they had one office on Central Wharf, near Montgomery street, and another at Clark's Point. Mr. Ellis has since filled the office of Sheriff for San Francisco. He has resided in New York at various times, but his time in that city has always been occupied in advancing the interests of California's vinicultural products.

Writing of Mr. Ellis' shipping office, reminds us of George W. Virgin, the shipping master, whose office was robbed by the Sydney thief, Jenkins, who was caught in the act, and hung. Mr. Virgin went from San Francisco to Siam, and became an Admiral in the Siamese Royal Navy, and a prime favorite with the Emperor, from whom he received distinguished consideration until his death. His Majesty made his favorite Admiral's obsequies a most imposing pageant.

Theodore C. Sanborn was of the firm of Gassett & Sanborn, on Jackson street wharf in '50. They were commission merchants, and lost largely in a great rice speculation. Many years afterward, we think in the Washoe excitement of '62–'63, Mr. Sanborn was fortunate, and paid thousands of dollars to his old creditors, notwithstanding time had released him from all legal responsibility. This we know, and record the fact with genuine pleasure.

Finley, Johnson & Co. were on the corner of Washington and Montgomery streets. J. W. Austin was of this firm.

Annan, Lord & Co. were at No. 275 Montgomery street.

L. W. Sloat, son of Commodore Sloat, was proprietor of the Merchants' Exchange, on the corner of Washington and Montgomery streets. Mr. Sloat was a conchologist, and had in his rooms a rare collection of shells.

Hiram B. Sherman was also on the corner of Montgomery and Washington.

Burgoyne & Co., bankers, were on the southwest corner of Washington and Montgomery. John V. Plume was a partner in this banking house. We are pleased to see Mr. Plume again in our streets, after so many years' absence.

Mazera N. Medina had an office on Montgomery, a little north of Washington street; and Medina, Hartog & Co. were on Washington, above Montgomery.

Middleton & Hood were auction and commission merchants, at 269 Montgomery street. The head of this firm was Mr. John Middleton, who is just as cool and self-controlled to-day as he was twenty-three years ago--moves, acts, speaks, and seems the same. We sincerely hope that another score of years may find him as he is to-day. Two doors from the store of Middleton & Hood, Harry Meiggs had his office, and we, with many others, believe San Francisco would have been none the loser were his office there to-day.

P. A. Morse, counselor-at-law, had his office on the corner of Washington and Montgomery. John Nugent's office was on Montgomery, between Washington and Clay.

Conroy & O'Connor were on Montgomery, north of Washington. John Rainey's store was on Montgomery, north of Washington.

James Dows & Co. were on, or next door to, the corner of Washington and Montgomery; and we seem to remember Mr. Phelps as a salesman for Dows & Co.—T. G. Phelps, who has since been Congressman for California, and Collector for the Port of San Francisco.

Beebe & Co. (S. Ludlow) were bankers on Montgomery, between Washington and Clay, in '50; and C. Marriott was a real estate broker close by. Edward S. Spear was a broker at 271 Montgomery street. Henry M. Naglee, since Gen. Naglee, was a banker on the corner of Merchant and Montgomery. Henry M. Naglee came to California as a Captain in Stevenson's

Regiment. Manrow & Co. (W. N. Meeks) were on Montgomery, near Washington. There are many men who were then in active business in San Francisco, whom we remember, and might mention; but we must not subside into a San Francisco Directory for the spring of '50.

Henry Meiggs was one of the most enterprising, generous and intelligent men who ever came to San Francisco, and his departure was one of the greatest losses that ever occurred to the city, in the taking of one individual from its population. The unfortunate complication and overwhelming liabilities which drove him from us, was a greater calamity to the prosperity of San Francisco than a conflagration or a flood. For him, personally, in a financial view, it was a great movement, and the tide which bore him through the "Golden Gate" "led on to fortune." Now, he is the Rothschild of Peru— the man to whom the Government applies in time of need, and not in vain; nor yet did any one ever personally apply to him for aid, or *for the settlement of any just debt*, without satisfaction. The tribute paid to Mr. Meiggs by the late Hon. Edward Tompkins, in a letter published in the San Francisco *News Letter*, was the reward from one good man to another. Every just claim presented to Mr. Meiggs has been liquidated; and the accusations made by some in authority against that gentleman after his departure, were utterly without foundation, but were of great convenience, just then, to some whom we all know to be *honorable men*.

Music, art, charity and society met with a great loss in the absence of Mr. Meiggs. The Music Hall, which stood where the Occidental Hotel now stands, was built by that gentleman. Mr. Leach, Mr. Beutler, Geo. Loder, Mrs. Wells, Miss Leach, Mr. Zander, and many other celebrities, came to California by the influence of Mr. Meiggs. The organ in Trinity Church was the gift of that gentleman. We believe no man ever went away from among us more sincerely regretted, and if he were to return, we are sure that his reception would be an ovation.

The wharf at North Beach, stretching so far into the harbor, was built by Mr. Meiggs, and is as much a feature of the city as the Plaza, or Montgomery street.

It was no inconsiderable undertaking in the early days to build such a pier; and now it is suggestive of what the builder might accomplish in our city, with to-day's facilities. Mr. Meiggs' departure from this city was an unfortunate mistake on his part, and still more unfortunate for the welfare of San Francisco. Had he remained with us, the false accusations which, by reason of his absence, certain people found it convenient to lay at his door, would have been traced then, as they since have been, to their proper source; and he would have long ago outlived his financial troubles, and won the confidence and esteem which his subsequently honorable career gives him in the minds of all just Californians. In South America, the munificence of his charities, and the grandeur of his operations in business, have made his name a proverb.

CHAPTER XXV.

In June, 1851, the citizens of San Francisco, who had long been smothering their indignation at the condition of things, superinduced by the lax administration of justice to criminals, were aroused to terrible action by the detection of a burglar in the very act of carrying off a portable safe, which he had just stolen from an office on Long Wharf. The property belonged to George W. Virgin, who had a shipping office, through the floor of which the burglar cut an entrance, took the safe—merely a big iron box—into his boat beneath the building, and pulled out into the bay. He was followed by several boats, containing men who had overheard him at his work, and when nearly overhauled, threw his booty overboard. Some of his pursuers hove to, and succeeded in grappling the sunken treasure and safely landing it, when it was identified. The other boats followed, and arrested the burglar after a short, desperate fight. He was taken to the rooms of the Vigilance Committee, and proved to be a Sydney thief named Jenkins, a low, brutal, foul-mouthed villain, of herculean frame, with thick, coarse red hair and beard. He was immediately tried, and convicted on indisputable testimony. He had been heard at his work, standing in his boat, cutting through the floor into the building; seen putting the safe into the boat; followed by men who never for a moment lost sight of him; observed to throw overboard the stolen property, which was subsequently raised and recognized; and finally captured.

All of this occurred early in the evening, and by the time the trial was finished and the sentence passed, it was midnight. The bell upon the engine house tolled out upon the quiet night—the preconcerted signal. Soon, a thousand men, ready and armed for action, had assembled. The doomed man, with pinioned arms, was marched out, along Sansome, California, Montgomery and Clay streets, to the Plaza. A proposition by some thoughtless person, to hang the condemned upon the flag-staff, was scorned as sacrilege, and the crowd moved on to the old adobe, which stood on the northwestern corner of the Plaza. Over a beam of the veranda, on the building's southern end, the rope was thrown—its other end already round the prisoner's neck, and when all was ready, the silent but determined crowd dragged him along the ground and off his feet, up to the beam. They held his body hanging there for hours, relays of men, relieving others, quiet and orderly, speaking in whispers.

There is something indescribably awful, and ominously thrilling, about a silent crowd of men in the darkness of night. Loud words of jest and laughter, or angry altercation, give explanation; but a dense crowd of silent men, standing, mysterious and alarmingly suggestive, or moving on, with that muffled tramp, so terrible and never to be forgotten, when heard from the feet of hurrying men with silent tongues, chills the listener's blood with dreadful apprehension. Jenkins, after his sentence, was asked to see a priest, which he declined, saying he would rather have a cigar; after which he requested some brandy and water. On the way to the gallows he spoke not a word. Arrived at the fatal spot, he refused, with obscenity and curses, the renewed offers of religious consolation, and died with ribaldry upon his lips. The night was moonlit, often obscured a moment by the passing clouds, bringing out, clearly defined, and then veiling in alternate light and charitable shade, the lifeless, hanging body, whose head and features, seen in "the phases of the moon," horribly grotesque, seemed nodding and grinning contemptuous defiance at his executioners.

Stuart, murderer as he was, had something almost redeeming, as he walked to death, looking, to the casual glance, no different from the other men, in whose ranks he walked erect and firm, with gleaming eye and unblanched face, dressed in a full suit of black, with every outward indication of a gentleman.

Watching the chances has been rewarded oftentimes by rich results in San Francisco. There are two rich men in this city, who accumulated the bulk of their wealth by watching for accidents in the business of other men; for omissions in legal documents; for little loopholes, wherein to insert one finger, until a larger orifice might be worn, and a lodgment obtained, from which to worry off the just and rightful owners, by bluffing, annoying, harassing, or, that failing, to compromise, *i. e.*, blackmail. When we say there are two, we must not be understood as saying there are only two, for doubtless there are scores of them; but this particular couple are, and have been for many years, under our especial observation, attracted first, many years ago, by a most cruel and treacherous act, which robbed a widow and several orphans, leaving them entirely destitute.

These men have emissaries constantly on the watch for any flaw in titles, any discrepancy in dates, any complication of circumstances, during which the crowding of claims, or pressure for payment, would ruin a man financially; which facts, brought to their knowledge, brings them down immediately on their prey. No home, no wife nor children, no domestic agony, are considered for a moment, when these men are legally enforced; and if the wrongs, the oppression, the ruined men and separated families, and all their wretchedness, through the rapacity of these two men, could be recorded, 'twould be a most damning record. They have never committed any act without the sanction of law. They are among our first citizens; they flaunt their wealth most arrogantly; but, as the old farmer said of one of his neighbors who was exceedingly blasphemous, boasting that his crop was in, all safely housed, without praying for the Divine aid he didn't want and didn't believe in, "Yes, yes, neighbor; but God doesn't settle with everybody in October!" And our two highly respected citizens still flourish.

Smaller rogues sometimes watch the chances,

with very profitable results—for the nonce; though no man or woman ever wronged another, without punishment equal to the offense, and without being conscious of it when the penalty came.

There was an English Jew in San Francisco in the early days, who was very plausible, courteous and respectable in appearance. What he did for a livelihood was not known or questioned, perhaps, as no one confined himself to one particular vocation. The merchant or the mechanic might follow, ostensibly, but one occupation, might be in his office or shop at just such stated hours as the merchant or mechanic of to-day; but he would be speculating in a dozen operations if they promised good profits, —and they mostly did then.

This Israelitish subject of H. B. M. formed the acquaintance of the Peralta family, and quite soon ingratiated himself in their favor. The native Californians were as unsuspecting as they were hospitable and honest, trusting implicitly their fellow-men. About that time, a sale of land on the Peralta tract brought in a large sum of money to its owner. The money was paid in gold coin, upon the counter of Palmer, Cook & Co's Bank, in the presence of Col. Hayes, Major Caperton and Mr. Cook, of the firm. The obsequious and solicitous friend was there, attending to the interests of El Señor Peralta, and advised him not to leave so large an amount in one bank, for fear of accidents; but to distribute it in fifty thousand dollar deposits in the various banking houses, which sage counsel was followed. The old gentleman did not notice that the amount placed in Davidson's Bank was on a certificate in favor of his officious friend. He did notice, however, that his attentive and constant visitor was absent after that day; and subsequently learned that he had drawn the deposit at Davidson's, and left on the first steamer for other climes.

The original owners of California lands were shamefully robbed, wronged and despoiled by squatters, and the thieving lawyers who set them to their work. The most infamous schemes were hatched by law firms in San Francisco, to rob the noblest, kindest men on the earth—the Rancheros of California. The recital of some facts would be of extreme interest to the public, and more exciting than pleasant to some of *our first citizens*.

Palmer, Cook & Co. were ever the friends of the old Spanish proprietors, aiding them with money and advice. Nearly all the great claims were settled through their house, unselfishly and honorably on their side, and in the best interests of their clients; and never, to our knowledge, was this banking firm anything else than an aid and help to all honest men seeking their coöperation.

Moses Ellis was of the firm of Ellis, Crosby & Co., on Sansome street, between Jackson and Pacific, in the spring of '50. Mr. Ellis was a very successful merchant, and left San Francisco a few years since to reside in some village in Massachusetts. We believe the California fever attacks him periodically, and we consider it a mere question of time as to when he shall succumb. We think that George Sanderson, who had been in Stockton since '49, came to San Francisco, and took Mr. Ellis' business on Front street, when the latter gentleman retired.

A. J. Ellis, who was at work one day in '49 near Montgomery and Jackson streets, ran a splinter under his nail, and on the spur, or the splinter of the moment, with that choleric impetuosity which is characteristic of him, threw his plane as far as he could into the open lot, now covered by the Metropolitan Theatre, vowing that he would never do another day's carpentering. He never has, and survives remarkably well.

There was a Mr. William Sharron in San Francisco in the spring of '50, who was a broker and commission merchant. He lived on the corner of Union and Mason streets. We do not know whether it was the gentleman who figures so prominently in the financial affairs of San Francisco to-day. We merely remember a gentleman of that name, and that he lived in the above mentioned place. We know that he is a man who has very little to say; but that he is heard from to considerable purpose occasionally, which induces us to believe that the Mr. Sharron of '73 and the Mr. Sharron of the spring of '50 are identical.

R. N. Berry was the lively broker, operator and commission merchant of those days; and subsequently, as long as his health permitted the exercise of his remarkable energies and fertile brain. Business to him was a mere pastime, like a recreation to ordinary men. Mr. Berry's management of business affairs was like the action of the painter, writer or advocate who has genius to aid his labors.

There were two brothers Sanchez, real estate brokers, on Clay street, above Montgomery, Bernardino and Santura. There was also a Joseph Sanchez, a broker, on Broadway, between Stockton and Dupont, but we do not know that he was a brother of the Clay street firm.

Robert Turnbull was a broker on Washington street; and J. Ambrose Hooper was in the same business on Jackson street. They were active, busy men.

James McIlwain was a wide-awake broker in those days, and is to-day; but he was a mere boy then, although he could sell merchandise with any of the men, and was a lively feature in the streets, rattling back and forth on his long-tailed, scampering pony. To-day, as in the spring of '50, his word is as good as his bond.

Asa and George Loring were manufacturing jewelers in San Francisco in '50. Whether they were of the firm of Loring & Hogg, in Ward's Court, or whether they were with Hayes & Lyndall, on Clay street, we are uncertain; but we do know that they were good craftsmen, and good citizens. Asa is long since dead. George worked in Grass Valley for many years since '51–'52, but is at present employed in the U. S. Mint at San Francisco.

Robert Shankland was of the firm of Shankland & Gibson, auctioneers, on Kearny, between Washington and Jackson. Mr. Shankland now leads a bucolic life, in company with Mr. James L. Riddle, near Mountain View.

The Hon. Thos. H. Selby was of the firm of Selby & Post, metal dealers, on Sacramento street, between Kearny and Dupont, in the spring of '50—active, shrewd and enterprising then as now.

Isaiah C. Woods, who was the manager of Adams & Co's banking house in San Francisco, was never understood or appreciated by the general public. He is one of the ablest business men ever in San Francisco. Had he been allowed to settle the affairs of Adams & Co., it would have been far better for the creditors of that firm. Mr. Woods is a man who would, in any other city than San Francisco, have been considered a valuable acquisition to its business men—its men of brains—its great movers and workers—and not only permitted, but requested to remain where he was—would have been aided and coöperated with, in continuing the house of Adams & Co.

Mr. Woods can originate any enterprise, clearly and feasibly, which, if carried out in detail, under his direction, will eventuate prosperously for the public and the projectors of the scheme. There was too much misrepresentation, prejudice and excitement at the time of the Adams & Co. failure; it was a very bad affair, but ought not to have been charged to I. C. Woods in all its disastrous mismanagement. Such men, with a fair chance, make business and prosperity for any city; and any such men's withdrawal, voluntary or compulsory, from business, is a public misfortune. We have always considered Mr. Woods as ranking in ability with I. Friedlander, W. C. Ralston, Jabez Howes, J. Palmer, Charles Cook, Harry Meiggs, and the late Henry Haight—men of broad, comprehensive vision, never forgetting the grand perspective, far-reaching to the horizon, because of some puny obstacle held temporarily before their eyes.

CHAPTER XXVI.

WHERE the Grand Hotel stands, on Market and Second streets, there was, in 1849, and up to 1853-4, a sand-hill, which was the subject of long and well-contested litigation, with strangely fluctuating fortune for the claimants on either side. It was taken to the Supreme Court and decided in favor of one party; a rehearing granted, and, after another long struggle, decided in favor of the other party. Then the ultimately successful ones were forced to hold it by force of arms. We remember Selim and Fred. Woodworth and Stephen Teschemacher arming and equipping themselves with shotguns, revolvers, sandwiches and stimulants, and encamping on the ground to hold possession against squatters, as late as 1853. In 1857 it was leased to Mr. Pease, brother of E. T. Pease, who occupied it as a coal-yard, at a merely nominal price, to hold possession for its owners. Although Second street was well built up on both sides, from Market to Rincon Hill, Market street, west of Second, was little more than a sand-waste. Father Maginnis' Church and a few straggling buildings were the only objects to mark the street line; and for a long time after Kearny was navigable to Market and across into Third street, there was a high sand-bank across Market, so high that the person walking from Kearny into Third, could not see the "Devisadero" heights, beyond the Mission. If we remember rightly, the obstruction remained there until excavated by the track-layers of the Market Street Railroad.

At the corner of O'Farrell and Dupont streets, in 1855-6, was a laundry; but the latter street was a *cul de sac*, unless you scaled the almost perpendicular sand-bank directly across the street, at the end of the laundry building, which feat accomplished, you saw a quiet valley, with a little, shallow *laguna*, a few cottages, and a garden and hot-houses of considerable dimensions, where Monsieur Habert cultivated exotics. The diminished domains of that garden still remain on Eddy street, near Powell, and a signboard informs the public that M. Vivien is the successor of M. Habert. This region was called St. Ann's Valley then, and the way to the Mission was easy for horses or pedestrians across this valley, the ground being generally firmer than round about it. As you went on, you saw a little church-belfry above the sand-hills; the same building now standing on the corner of Geary and Mason, and used at present as a school-house. A big sand-hill stood where Starr King's Church, the City College, and the blocks of buildings on both sides of Stockton, between Geary and O'Farrell, now stand.

A large wooden house, the residence of Dr. Gates, stood on the hill at the southwest corner of Geary and Stockton; as high —the ground floors of it—as the roof of the College building on the opposite corner now is from the present street level. In '59 or '60 this building was lowered and placed on the Geary street line, where it now stands, occupied by Dr. Calvert, dentist. In '60 and '61 Mr. Ohm, the importer of watches for so many years in this city, came to live in the cottage adjoining the building last mentioned, and soon after purchased the fifty-vara lot in the centre of the block, on the Geary street line, and erected the four commodious dwellings now thereon. Long after this time, the Union Plaza-ground was covered by a sand-hill, so high that the neighbors on the surrounding streets could see only the roofs of the houses opposite their own.

Near the corner of Powell and Geary, on the latter street, was a three-story wooden building, used as a laundry. The same building is now on Powell, just below Geary, on the east side of the street, and now answers for a double house. Where Dr. Hemphill's Church now stands, there was a single story cottage and stables, occupied by the owner of the property. A pretty little girl with flaxen curls used to live there; and often, when we passed that way, she put her tiny hands through the railing of the fence, for us to shake, and wish her "Good morning!"

Where the Scotch Presbyterian Church stands, on Mason street, near Eddy, there stood, until three or four years ago, the house of Henry Gerke, the great viniculturist.

Mr. Gerke built on this spot in 1847, more than a year before the discovery of gold in digging the Sutter mill-race. The Gerke House was a capacious wooden building, two stories, with a high roof, and broad, sheltering verandas on both stories—a comfortable, homelike dwelling. We used to look upon this house with peculiar feelings of regard and interest years ago, when passing it; standing solitary among the sand-hills, so remote from even the little city which was itself so far away from all the rest of busy human kind. It seemed so strange a place to build a home—away from all society, out of sight of every human habitation—so still by day and lonesome after nightfall, year after year—until gregarious mankind approached, with steady creeping tide of population, until its flood surrounded them on every side, and Fate or Chance, as if resenting the long and silent isolation of that old home, built on the very spot a church, where hundreds now meet in congregation, and raise their voices in loud united praise and songs of thanksgiving.

The Waverly House was a large, four-story wooden building, on the north side of Pacific street, between Montgomery and Kearny. It was painted a dark brown, and the words "Waverly House" painted in huge white letters upon its front. It was very well conducted, and quite a comfortable place, at five dollars per diem, per capita. The house stood upon an uneven portion of the street, and the platform before the entrance was, at its eastern end, raised but two or three steps above the ground, while, at the western extremity of the hotel front, it ended twelve feet above the ground, without rail or guard of any kind. We remember an invalid passenger (a Mr. Chapman) who arrived in June, '50, being sufficiently recovered to take a little evening exercise on the platform, walked back and forth a few times in the dark, and then, thinking to extend his promenade round the corner, walked off, severely injuring himself, and prolonging his stay at the "Waverly."

The hill, up Clay street to the postoffice, on the corner of Pike and Clay, was very steep in the spring of '50. The Plaza was an open, uninterrupted space, from the buildings on Clay street to those on Washington street. Steps were cut into the ground along where the sidewalk now borders the Plaza, and in some places on the opposite side—quite an aid in climbing for letters at the postoffice. Colonel Geary opened the first postoffice on the corner of Washington and Montgomery; thence he removed to the corner of Washington and Stockton; thence to the corner of Pike and Clay. Here, long lines of patient men, six and twelve months from home, *via* Cape Horn, waited for letters. The looker-on could see happy faces and sad ones turning away from the windows, whence issued sealed missives more portentous than the contents of Pandora's box! The window-clerks rarely, if ever, had change for a dollar, and the happy recipient of a letter cared nothing at such a moment for his change.

It was said that some fellows made quite a good salary by selling out, when near the window, to some new comer, with more money than patience. In 1851, the postoffice was removed to the zinc-covered building on the northeast corner of Dupont and Clay, the western half of which house was occupied at the same time by E. Wilson, as a restaurant. Mr. Wilson afterward opened Wilson's Exchange, now the American Exchange, on Sansome, near Sacramento street. We never pass these old postoffice neighborhoods, without imagining the air peopled with invisible beings, haunting the spot where they were born of joys and sorrows, engendered in the hearts of men, excessively emotional.

The first brick building on California street was erected for Fitzgerald, Bausch & Brewster, who were, prior to that time, on Sacramento street. This brick building stood where the California market now stands. Where Mr. Stevenson's large brick building now stands, on the southwest corner of California and Montgomery streets, Leidesdorff's cottage stood in 1849. It was a one-story building, with a pyramidal kind of roof. The front of the house faced the east as nearly as any point, for it stood diagonally on the lot. There were two windows and a door in the front; the door was reached by a little flight of steps to a platform, with a railing. There was a railed enclosure, commencing at the Montgomery street south end of the house, and the west end on California street. There was a large wooden building on this corner in '50 or '51. Payne & Dewey had an auction and sales room in the lower story. John Middleton also had an auction room in the same place. Clayton once kept a restaurant, called the "Jackson House," in the same building. Madame Martin, since of the Maison Doré, N. Y., used to keep lodging rooms in this house.

A sketch of Montgomery street, by Pendergast, showing the front of this building, and Chinamen at work in the erection of Parrott's stone building, now occupied by Wells, Fargo & Co., may be seen at Barry & Patten's. The stone for the Parrott building was dressed and fitted in China. The tenants of Mr. Stevenson's building accord its owner the reputation of being the most obliging landlord in the city; and it is generally understood that the building pays the best interest of any property on Montgomery street, and Mr. Stevenson's tenants do not like to look farther and fare worse.

Hull & Ryckman were the proprietors of the "New World" building, on the northeast corner of Commercial and Leidesdorff. The lower floor was a large saloon, and the upper stories were offices and lodging rooms. We remember that a man who had been employed in the building, painting, papering, or doing something else, was remonstrated with by Mr. Ryckman for negligence or dishonesty in his work, when he became insolent, saying to Mr. Ryckman, "If you were a younger man I would whip you." "Oh, don't let that deter you in the least," said Mr. Ryckman, getting up from his chair, and closing the office door. "I'll not ask any odds on that account," he continued, walking up to the man and giving him a rousing box on the ear. The man exerted himself with all his ability, but was soon compelled to succumb, and gladly departed when Mr. Ryckman pointed to the door.

Nash, Patten & Thayer built and owned the "Kremlin," on the southeast corner of Commercial and Leidesdorff. The lower floor was occupied by a saloon, bar and restaurant, and the upper floors by lodging rooms. The restaurant was on the Leidesdorff side of the building. It was on the beach, in the rear of this building, where Captain Folsom shot Mr. Nathaniel Page

—or Mr. Page's watch—as the ball struck the time-keeper, which foiled the death-dealer. This assault took place on the beach, nearer to Halleck street than Commercial, but it was all open water outside Leidesdorff street. The tide came up under the "New World" and "Kremlin" buildings, as late as May 4th, when both houses were destroyed by fire.

John H. Redington was of the firm of E. S. Holden & Co., druggists, on Sansome, between California and Pine, in 1850. Subsequently Mr. Redington was with Andrew J. Almy, on the southeast corner of Clay and Montgomery. Dr. Holden has since resided in Stockton, and been Mayor of that town. He is a very active railroad man, with views and energy far in advance of that dozing village by the San Joaquin. Mr. Redington has been in the California Senate. Mr. Almy died some years since, and W. H. Keith occupied the old store on the corner of Clay and Montgomery for some time prior to removing across the street, into Howard's building, now occupied by James G. Steele & Co.

CHAPTER XXVII.

In the summer of 1850 we lived in a little cottage on Montgomery street, somewhere between Broadway and Vallejo; the precise spot we cannot tell, as there were no land-marks to designate street lines, the whole neighborhood being precipitous, rough and uneven, save where some little space had been leveled for a house or tent. There were very few habitations of any kind, after passing the line of Broadway.

Nearly opposite our domicile was a little tent, its only occupants, a woman and child. The mother was seldom seen; the daughter, a delicate, interesting child of eight or nine years, was often at the opening of the tent, shyly observing us, with childlike curiosity, as we went down to the city in the morning and returned at evening. The mother and child were dressed in poor, soiled, mourning garments, but their attire could not make them seem coarse or unrefined. In the occasional glimpse of the mother, we could discern the unmistakable lady—that something which all can see and none describe. We never spoke with her, knew nothing of her, not even her name; but knew she was a well-bred, accomplished lady. She had a poor, jingley, old piano in her wretched, little canvas apology for a shelter; but she never indulged in any trashy music. Early in the morning and late in the evening we heard her practising, with the facility and grace of a musician—a style which even the muffling canvas could not hide. Sometimes, though seldom, she gave a little scrap of a sonata, a fragment of Mozart, Beethoven or Sebastian Bach, with exquisite effect, but never any trash.

In our daily and constant going and coming, we made friends with the little, lonesome-looking girl, so pale and quiet; and she was always watching for us, morning and night—a pure pleasure for us, so far from home and children. We often brought her some trifle—a toy, a little paper of confectionery, a cake or picture-book, which she received at first shyly, but with much pleasure; and after our better acquaintance, with an unconcealed delight, that made the moment as much to us as to her poor little fragile self—worth all the day beside. One evening at our return we missed her, and lingered awhile to meet her, but she did not come.

We went in to our dinner, but the little omission had made us less hungry than usual, and we dwelt upon our little friend's absence long into the evening.

When morning came she was not there to welcome us, and we waited vainly, almost determined to step to the tent and satisfy our curiosity; but did not—turning down the hill, with reluctant steps, to our daily labor. We thought, all through the long September day, about our little friend, sure of meeting her when we went home; but again we were disappointed, and resolved to know in the morning all about our missing one. We questioned our host and his wife, but they had not noticed—believed they had seen neither mother nor child that day. At midnight we were awakened by a woman's voice in agony of weeping, and supplicating prayer. Starting from our bed, we hastened to the window. All was still; not a sound came to our listening ears. The moon was wonderfully bright, revealing every object in the still, cool night, with great distinctness.

Thinking we had been awakened by a dream, we were turning back to bed, when a loud cry rang out upon the silent night—a wail so utterly despairing, that our heart stood still.

It came from the little tent; there was a dull, reddish light through the canvas, unnoticeable before in the all-powerful moonlight. Agonizing sobs followed the long, thrilling cry; the mother's voice calling her darling's name; the sound of oft-repeated kisses; then low moans and silence. The child was dead! We hastily dressed and hurried to the spot. There were other voices in the tent; soft, soothing words from women's lips and from their hearts—kind, sympathizing neighbors, we knew, by the lighted, open doors near by. Knowing the poor, motherless woman was in gentle hands, we turned sadly away to wait for daylight. We longed to offer some sympathy or assistance; but it never would have helped the wretched mother, who was almost paralyzed with grief.

As we went down our daily path, our heart heavy with its first sorrow in this earthly paradise, we met a man carrying a little coffin on his shoulder. Stopping in the path, we stood uncovered, repeating in our heart, "The Lord giveth and the Lord taketh away: blessed be the name of the Lord!" and went on to the battle of life, with no courage in our heart. When we came home at night, the place seemed strangely altered. A little, level place on the hillside, was all that remained to mark the spot where had been the tent, our innocent little friend, the mother's long days of anxious poverty, and her last night of hopeless agony. They were gone from our sight and knowledge, from everything but memory, forever.

CHAPTER XXVIII.

The late James Donahue was one of the most practical men and useful citizens ever known in San Francisco. His great energies were always directed towards some object which ultimately resulted in public improvement and the welfare of his fellow citizens. His sagacity and foresight are proven by the eventuating of his undertakings. Having once conceived an enterprise, it was viewed on every side in the searching light of his strong practical sense; and when determined upon, was persistently pursued to sure success. His worldly wisdom was only equaled by his modesty and charity; and we may truly say that, among all the men whom we remember, during the almost quarter of a century of our life in San Francisco, we recall not one more moral, useful and upright citizen than the late James Donahue.

Mr. Joseph G. Eastland was in San Francisco in 1849, but we do not place him, until '52 or '53, when he was with the S. F. Gas Co. Mr.

Eastland was the confidential secretary of the late James Donahue, who was a man to select none but good officers. In brief, to any one acquainted with the late Mr. Donahue, this fact is as good as many elaborated pages upon the character and qualifications of Mr. Eastland, who is indeed a gentleman of refined and cultivated tastes, aside from his thorough business capacity.

Dr. Parker—W. C. Parker—was of the firm of Stevenson & Parker, in 1850. Their office was in the adobe building, on the Plaza. They were in the real estate business. Col. Stevenson was the commander, and Dr. Parker was the surgeon of Stevenson's Regiment. We do not think there is a man in California who has any just cause of complaint against Dr. W. C. Parker. Not that he is a negative character, by any means, or a person who will bear the least crowding; but he is so quiet, so unassuming, and still so perfectly just in all his dealings, that we cannot believe any one knows him without coinciding with our expressed opinion.

Colonel Stevenson is too well known for any remarks in our pages. We would like to have the secret of the Colonel's unflagging vigor and vitality. We were turning into a doorway on Montgomery street, a short time since, to visit one of the up-stairs offices; and, as we were walking up, Colonel Stevenson brushed past us, with a cheery "Good morning!" and jumped up, two steps at a time, to the landing, like a school-boy. Most of our citizens conform a little to the fashions, but the Colonel wears the same style of closely-buttoned frock, and military fatigue cap; and seems the same Colonel Stevenson who came here in 1847.

There was a Dr. Parker, who had an office on Kearny street in '49, and in June, '50; but we do not remember seeing him since that time. He was a tall, large-framed man, with a long, dark beard; and we remember hearing him say that he was from Shirley, Mass., and think he was a graduate of old Harvard.

James L. King arrived in San Francisco on the steamer *Tennessee*, June 20th, 1850. We believe that Captain Cole commanded the *Tennessee* that trip. Lieut. McDermott, of the U.S.N., was her first officer; and subsequently was on the *Alta's* editorial staff. Mr. King has been a successful real estate operator, and is exceedingly well posted on any titles to land within six miles of the Plaza. Our intercourse has always been pleasant, and we are indebted to Mr. King for many valuable items.

S. F. Blaisdell is one of the California pioneers. We believe he came from Lima to San Francisco. To the former city he went as engineer of the steamer *Rimac*, which was built in the United States, and sent out for the Peruvian Government in 1847. Mr. Blaisdell has long been interested in one of the first established telegraph companies of San Francisco. He is a man of strong predilections and emphatic expression, but of true and sterling integrity.

Fred. Thibault was a commission merchant at 245 Montgomery street, in the spring of '50. But we have known him so many years in his official capacity, that it is a little difficult to believe that he could ever have been anything else than the most exact of conveyancers and public notaries. To be on the spot "where men most do congregate," and not see Mr. Thibault's well known figure and peculiar *sombrero*, would be a strange incident in that day.

William H. Tillinghast, now a banker on California street, was, in the spring of '50, of the firm of E. Mickle & Co., on Clay street, north side, between Montgomery and Sansome. Mr. Tillinghast came from Valparaiso to San Francisco. He is a thorough-bred merchant and a courteous gentleman.

Samuel Price was of the firm of E. D. Heatley & Co., commission merchants, on Exchange Court, off Montgomery street. Mr. Price was the consul for Chili in the spring of '50, and, if we are not mistaken, is a native of that country. However, we are sure that no more amiable man in business, or the social relations of life, ever came to San Francisco from any part of the world.

R. H. Sinton arrived in California on board the U. S. ship of war *Ohio*, Commodore Jones, in 1847. Mr. Sinton was acting paymaster, the purser having become insane on the passage. In the spring of '50, Mr. Sinton was of the firm of Sinton & Bagley, on Clay, below Kearny street, their store being on the same spot now occupied by Lewis' jewelry store. In all the years of Mr. Sinton's residence in San Francisco, in his business relations, his official capacity and social life, he has had the respect and confidence of his fellow-citizens. Mr. Sinton is now in the real estate business with Gen. Geo. P. Ihrie, late of the U. S. A.

Phillip McGovern was on the corner of First and Mission streets, in the days when first we knew him—some time in '50; and in all the time since those days, we have known nothing but good of him. We meet him occasionally, and he wears well. We hope he may be with us for many years to come.

Charles Lux had his office on Kearny street, near Sacramento, in 1850; and, if we are not mistaken, is in the same place to-day. Not the same building—a large brick building stands where the old wooden structure containing Mr. Lux's office stood, twenty-three years ago. What shabby old shanties made up Kearny street in those days! We were all in a hurry then; we didn't think so much of appearances as now—hadn't time! Now, Kearny street is quite urban; and our old friend Lux has "cattle upon a thousand hills."

Mr. Thomas Breeze, of the firm of Murphy, Grant & Co., was at a desk in an office on Clay street wharf, the first time we ever saw him. It was on the ninth of June, 1850; and we remember, also, that Elisha W. Bourne and Captain Brenham, subsequently Mayor of San Francisco, were at Mr. Breeze's desk, on business. We know of few men who have given themselves so unremittingly to business for the past twenty-three years as Mr. Breeze; and we are glad in our belief that he has reaped the reward of his long labors.

John F. Lohse was a merchant on Washington street, between Montgomery and Sansome, in the spring of '50, and was an agreeable man with whom to transact business. He still retains that amiable trait, and will to-day negotiate with affable courtesy the sale of powder enough to blow up every truant husband in the State of California. Music is a grand conservant of men's lives and tempers, and Mr. Lohse is one of the *dilettante*.

Camilo Martin was on Washington street, between Montgomery and Sansome, in the spring of '50. To-day, Mr. Martin is the consul for Spain, and is in the London and San Francisco Bank. As we see Mr. Martin passing along the street to-day, he appears the same as he did twenty-three years ago.

Mr. William Stevenson, so long the treasurer of Maguire's Opera House, arrived in San Francisco in 1849. Soon after his arrival, Mr. Rowe opened his circus entertainments on Kearny street, exactly where Commercial street now opens into it; and Mr. Stevenson took charge of the financial department. Through all the years since that time, and in the various places of amusement where our old friend has counted so much of "the root of all evil," we may venture to state that the cash always balanced, to the satisfaction of all parties concerned.

Grayson & Guild were on the east side of

Sansome, between Pacific and Jackson; and in the summer of '50, there was just room enough to drive drays past their store-door; the bank rising abruptly along the line of the middle of the street in front of their store, making the western half of the way nearly as high as the roof of their building. A. J. Grayson and family are painted in Jewett's picture of "The California Pioneer." Mr. Guild, we believe, returned to St. Louis many years ago. Mr. J. F. Lightner, who was with Grayson & Guild at this time, is still a resident, and, we think, is in business on California street.

Norton, Satterlee and Norton were counselors-at-law, and had their office in No. 1, Laffan's Building, Plaza. The late Hon. Edward Norton, Chief Justice of California, and Myron Norton, were the partners of Judge Satterlee, who was Judge of the Superior Court in '52–'53. The late David C. Broderick used to-say: "We are sure of justice in the Superior Court, because John Satterlee sits there." Nathaniel Bennett was an Associate Justice of the Supreme Court at that time. The McAllisters, father and son, were eminent lawyers at that time. Hall McAllister always has plenty of business, because he never neglects his clients. Edwards, Chetwood, Rose, Pringle, Whitcomb, Noyes,

Lake, Janes, Boyd, Barber, and many others, were practising law in San Francisco in the spring of '50. Ogden Hoffman's office was also in Laffan's building in '50.

We have elsewhere spoken of Dr. Jones and his eccentric conduct with his gold-dust; but we omitted to mention the fact of his going home to ———, we forget the town, in New York State, but think it was Poughkeepsie, his native place—somewhere in that neighborhood, however—and taking his treasure with him. He would not have it out of his sight; refused to deposit or invest it; but kept it in his room, and sat watching it all day and nearly all night; too anxious to slumber—afraid to close his eyes, lest his treasure should "take to itself wings." Of course this could not long continue; and soon the insomnious argonaut died midst his golden fleece.

Fred Gibbs, Morton Cheesman, Capt. Johns, and Florence Mahoney, arrived on the steamship *California*, January 22, 1850. Mr. Gibbs' first place of business was on Washington street, near Kearny; then on Sansome, corner of Washington, where he was burned out; and was again and again burned out on Sansome street—three times in all. Mr. Gibbs is a generous, warm-hearted man and true friend; a good citizen, and a graduate of old Harvard.

Morton Cheesman is a good specimen of the men of '50—not half a century, he's a young man yet—and is widely and favorably known in business and social circles. Capt. Johns arrived twenty-two days too late for the Association of Pioneers; but, for all that, they elected him their president, one foggy evening, much to the astonishment of many worthy citizens, who were here two or three weeks prior to Captain Johns' arrival, yet believed themselves ineligible. The next morning, when the fog had cleared away, the brilliant body who had elevated Captain Johns to the presiding chair of their august assembly, looked very solemn, and conferred in anxious whispers, the result of which was a reconsideration of their vote, which let Captain Johns out of the Association of Pioneers.

This unparliamentary action was more amusing than surprising to the citizens of San Francisco, who knew of the prevailing fog about the heads. Some day, a good healthy breeze will clear up the heavy mists, and make it plain sailing for all Californians who were here on the ninth of September, 1850. Florence Mahony died long years ago, and all our recollections of him are pleasant. All the partners in his firm—Case, Heiser & Co.—are dead.

CHAPTER XXIX.

William Shear was the proprietor of the "Tontine," on the southeast corner of Montgomery and Commercial, in 1849-50. In September, '51, Mr. Shear took the Nightingale Hotel, at the Mission. Tenbroeck & Clark opened the "Nightingale" in 1850.

Mr. Shear is in some respects a very remarkable man. His great fund of vitality and exuberance of spirits, health and endurance, are simply wonderful. His quick, keen perception of the situation, and his ability to master it, to make troubled elements harmonious, is nothing less than genius. So many men past youth become morose or misanthropic, that it cheers one to meet an *old boy* like Mr. Shear. Personally, he seems as active and vigorous as in the spring of '50; mentally, just as ready in repartee, in fun and humor; still firm in the belief that happiness is the principal thing in this world; and certainly he is a very good illustration of its value as a sanitary proposition.

One evening we were in company with a convivial party, among whom were Harry B——— and Tom F———. They were very jolly, and as usual, disposed to ventilate their classics. After numerous quotations, correct and very much mixed, they came to a snag—not literal —but literary. They tried, and stuck upon it; tried again and again, but with no better success, until it was too evident that the professed *belle lettre* men couldn't make the connection. At this juncture, Bill Shear, who had been leaning back, silently smoking through all the mountain labor, said: "Why, I am surprised, gentlemen! I supposed, at first, that you were joking—here's the quotation!" He gave it correctly, adding, "I knew that I could shoe a horse better than any of you; but I never for one moment imagined I could beat you at your own game."

Thomas J. Poulterer was on the corner of California and Montgomery street in 1849–50. We remember a great sale of China goods, fancy furniture, bedsteads, lounges, chairs, work-tables, silks, shawls, ivory-work, stoneware, etc., seemingly enough to supply the whole city for a year. Mr. Poulterer is great as an auctioneer; he establishes a sympathy between his audience and himself as soon as he commences to speak, which makes his sales successful. There is nothing narrow or mean in his nature, and he makes himself deservedly popular, without the slightest intention.

Mr. Poulterer, after rusticating for a while beneath the shade of his own vine and fig-tree, in the salubrious air of Sonoma, where George Watriss, C. V. Stewart and Major Snyder now reside, has returned to our midst, where we hope he may long live and prosper.

William F. Williamson, Willis Johnson and Samuel Davis built the "Veranda," on the corner of Washington and Kearny streets, in June, 1850, and were doing a fine business there until Willis Johnson's death, which interrupted the smooth flow of fortune's tide, and Mr. Williamson went to Gold Bluff, subsequently to Downieville, and later still to Sonora, Tuolumne county. The Bay View Park Hotel was opened by Mr. Williamson, and kept in better style than any "out-of-town hotel" ever opened in California. It was glorious for the guests, but not remunerative to Mr. Williamson, who has, since leaving the "Bay View," been the Turf Reporter for the "Alta California." No man in California, perhaps none in America, has a more voluminous record of Turf Sports than

Mr. Williamson, who is quoted as authority in those matters.

Frederick Marriott was in business with a Mr. Anderson, as monetary agents, in Cross, Hobson & Co's building, on Clay street, in 1849. Mr. Marriott was at that time the correspondent of the *London Times*. Subsequently he was with Smith Brothers in the "Exchange for All Nations," on the corner of Sansome and California; and still more recently in business with Mr. Alfred Wheeler. For many years Mr. Marriott has been the proprietor of the *News Letter*, which has grown to be a very popular and profitable institution, having amongst its contributors the ablest pens in California. This paper numbers more Atlantic subscribers than any other newspaper on the Pacific coast, and is found on the reading-room tables of every first class Club in London.

Alexander Austin, our present Tax Collector, had a bakery on Pacific street, in the latter part of '49 or the spring of '50. In '52, perhaps earlier, Mr. Austin opened his dry goods store, on Sacramento street, just above Montgomery. Subsequently he removed to Montgomery, between Sacramento and California; and later still, to the corner of Sutter and Montgomery.

Mr. Austin has been twice elected to the office of Tax Collector, with satisfaction to all parties. He is a true friend, and full of charity and kindness. It has always been a kind of proverb or standing joke, that the Scotch are a close-fisted, stingy nation. We never were in the "land o' cakes," but if the Scotch are so at home, the climate of California has a wonderful effect upon them, for they are the most liberal people in our country. Messrs. Alexander and Joseph Austin, Donald McClellan, James Laidley, the Watt brothers, Mr. Chisholm, the late James Murray and George Gordon, in fact, all of the Scotchmen we have known in San Francisco, have been liberal, public-spirited men. Donald McClellan is a good specimen of the Scotch-American; a shrewd, active, liberal-minded business man; open-handed and generous, always developing the resources of any country where he may be living, and making employment for many men.

The *California Courier*, a daily paper, was published and edited by Crane & Rice. T. J. Dryer was city editor and reporter. The office was on Montgomery street, near the Custom House.

Nugent & Co. were the proprietors of the

Daily Herald. John Nugent was the editor. Office on Montgomery, between Clay and Washington. Subsequently the *Herald* office was on Montgomery, a little south of Sacramento.

The *Journal of Commerce,* a daily paper, was published by Washington Bartlett. Office, Montgomery street, between Washington and Clay.

The *Pacific News* office was on Kearny, between Pacific and Jackson. Its proprietors were J. Winchester and R. N. Allen. J. Winchester, editor.

The *Evening Picayune*, a daily paper, was published by Gihon & Co. Peter A. Brinsmade was its editor. The *Picayune* office was on Jackson, between Kearny and Montgomery.

The *Watchman*, a monthly, religious paper, was edited by Albert Williams, in the *Journal of Commerce* office.

C. L. Taylor's office was on Dupont street, between Pine and California. He was a lumber and commission merchant, the same as to-day, and, as to-day, liberal, enterprising, charitable and public spirited.

Henry Wetherbee was on Pacific street, between Sansome and Battery.

Henry Pierce was the proprietor of the Eagle Bakery, on Stockton street, between Green and Union.

George C. Potter was Assistant City Surveyor, at City Hall.

Endicott, Greene & Oakes were merchants on Central Wharf. Mr. Greene has since been of the firm of Greene, Heath & Allen.

Probst, Smith & Co. were merchants on California street, between Montgomery and Sansome.

Hastler, Baine & Co. were on California street, between Montgomery and Sansome. Mr. McKnight, so many years with the latter firm, is now in Davidson's Bank, on the corner of Commercial and Montgomery.

At the head of the medical profession in San Francisco, in the spring of '50, were Dr. Bowie, Dr. Stout, Dr. H. M. Gray, Dr. S. R. Gerry, Dr. Bertody, Dr. McMillan, and Drs. Coit, S. R. Harris, Turnbull, Tewksbury, Bennett, Mackintosh and Rowell. Many of these gentlemen are still in practice in San Francisco—all of them men of intellectual superiority and unusual attainments. There were many others in San Francisco, but personally unknown to us. Dr. Stackpole, Dr. May, Dr. Sturtevant, Dr. Megguier, Drs. West, Forbes, White, Whitfield, Trescott, Gihon, Franklin, Grover, Barstow, Gates, Shuler, Morgan, D. S. Smith, Parker, O'Brien, Morrison, Pierce, Dr. Moore, and Dr. Miller, all in practice in San Francisco in the spring of '50. We do not remember the exact time when Dr. Dupuytren, Dr. Badarous, Doctors Cole, Whitney, Eckel, Toland, Sawyer, Bruner, Burgess, Fourgeaud, and other eminent men, came to this city, but we are confident that it was subsequent to the spring of '50.

CHAPTER XXX.

Whenever we go out on the Presidio road, or on the much traveled drive to the "Cliff," and reach that point of observation which takes in the abrupt shores forming the northern boundary of the "Golden Gate," the sight of those precipitous reddish-brown headlands, looking as if sliced off—split away by some Titan's axe—always puts us in a speculative vein—a wondering mood—a wish to know when that mighty bulk of rock and mountain height was rent away from the Coast Range, permitting the passage inland of the waves that had for ages chafed, and foamed, and fretted for admission. There is a kind of recent look about the cleft wall of the "Contra Costa" side of the harbor's entrance—recent, geologically speaking; but we are no geologists. Hugh Miller could not, we imagine, possibly conceive of a human being, possessing an average intelligence, who knew so little of the earth's formation as we confess to; but we have never looked over at the Marin shore without feeling more and more convinced that, in 1578-9, the salt ocean did not flow where we now see the white-winged messengers pass to and fro. We say 1578-9 because, at that time, Sir Francis Drake—or, more correctly speaking, Captain Drake, at that time, afterward Sir Francis—wintered with his crew, at what is now known as Drake's Bay; and it is not probable that, if the harbor had been in existence then, he would not have taken possession, or at least explored it and given it a name.

To those who say, "Oh, Drake passed it in the fog—navigators do it now, every month in the year in which fogs prevail," we will reply that Captain Drake's log says: "We followed the shore *on foot*, southward, one hundred miles, etc.," describing the climate, soil, general appearance, until they "came to a river flowing into the sea." Now, that river's outlet must have been some sixty miles south of San Francisco's present location—that river poured the waters of the Sacramento and the San Joaquin into the Pacific. There might have been an inland lake, lying all the way where the Bay now stretches, from San Francisco's northern extremity to San José. It is more reasonable to believe that a great convulsion of Nature formed the Golden Gate since Drake was here, than that there was a harbor here then, and he did not discover it. Long after Drake's day came the great French navigator, La Perouse. He never found a harbor where we now see the heaving tide bearing the "richly freighted argosies." Nor did any one ever know or suspect its existence until about a century ago, when the Franciscan friars, traveling up from Mexico to found their missions still farther north, came upon the headlands at what is now known as Point Lobos, and looking down upon the leaping breakers on the Bar, saw that which no civilized man had ever before seen—the grandest harbor between Puget Sound and Cape Horn. We have always believed that the Franciscan friars were the discoverers of the Golden Gate; that they were the first of civilized men who looked upon the result of that awful convulsion which rent the mountains and sank them in the exulting ocean's mouth, whose foaming, trembling lip ceaselessly frets along the rocky shore, as if in hungry anticipation of another greedy swallow out of the opposing body of its natural enemy. As we look upon the huge fracture on the northern sea wall, built by Earth's architect, we can imagine the fearful throes of Mother Nature—the awful subterranean thunders, the grinding of sunken rocks and roar of engulfing waters, the clouds of blinding dust, the wild flight of terrified birds, and dreadful consternation of every living thing within the scope of its paralyzing action.

Always, as we look upon the swelling tide at the harbor's mouth, the ocean seems like some huge, breathing, conscious animal, panting yet with the pride of its achievement, but too unwieldy and gigantic ever again to be composed and calm until the lapse of centuries.

Often, in years gone by, we used to hear from the early settlers of the country adjacent to San Francisco (then "Yerba Buena"*) of a tradition among Indians that, many, many years ago, their forefathers went down from their homes above where we now live, to attend a great festival somewhere near the present site of Monterey—and that, while there, a terrible earthquake occurred. When they were returning to their homes, they found the old pathway abruptly ended at a jagged cliff, from whose precipitous edge they gazed with wonder at a flowing sea beneath their feet; then turned and wound their toilsome way far round the Contra

---

*Good Herb. "Yerba Buena," an aromatic herb growing at that time on the hills of the present city's site.

Costa side. "Never, since that day," says the legend, "has the Devil's Mountain (Monte Diablo) spit forth fire and smoke."

THE FARALLONES. — A little surf-washed and storm-beaten group of rocky islets; not large enough to be dignified by the term islands, yet standing so firm against the great Pacific Ocean's long swell, that, rising off the shores of Japan, never ceases until it leaps in snowy foam and thunders in angry rage against this sturdy little outpost of the great continent that bars its further progress. How few among the one hundred and seventy thousand—*mas o menos*—inhabitants, who every morning enjoy their regular coffee and *Alta*, have any idea of the Farrallones, within thirty miles of where they spin out their thread of life? How many dwellers in the Chrysopolis can tell you how many millions of dozen of murr's eggs have been taken from these rocky rookeries since the year 1849? How many are there who know the meaning of the word Farall? Velesquez's Spanish dictionary says: Farallon—a cliff, a cape, a headland, a pointed island in the sea. Some have thought it meant the island of the Lion (Leone), Farall Leone. Some Spaniards say Farall is lantern, beacon, lighthouse. There is a gigantic monolith upon these rocks, with an immense, clean-cut, round hole, like the window, or light in a lantern, through which the setting sun glows with peculiar effect. Some say that from this the name is derived. The lighthouse beams its welcome beacon to the fog-bewildered mariner from the topmost point of these rocks now; but it is not likely that any lanterns were ever hung there before, since the place was known to man, by land or sea. But it is not with the name that we have now to do—'tis with the dwellers upon this lonely little outpost—the countless myriads of sea-birds—the Murre, or Muir, as it is vulgarly called—the "*Uria Californica,*" as classed by ornithologists. No description can give the reader any conception of the numbers of these birds thronging this spot, perching upon every possible foothold, every projection where a lodgment can be obtained; crowding the pinnacles and ridges; squeezing into every hollow and aperture; innumerable as blades of grass. In one place known as the Great Rookery—a hollow, or little valley—the birds are so densely packed that, save at the outskirts of the crowd, nothing but the heads of the birds can be seen. So closely do they crowd together, that their heads, in uniformity of size and color, seem like a vast bed of pebbles agitated by some subterranean commotion; and it is almost an impossibility for one of them to rise upon his wings or extricate himself from the entanglement, unless he be one of the outer ones.

They live upon fish, and may be truly said to earn their living, as well as any of the hardy Italians who sally out in all weathers, and seem as industrious and fearless in capturing their prey, as the feathered dwellers of these little islets. The Murre's egg is rather larger than the ordinary hen's egg; of a dim, turquoise blue, spotted with black. They are rather strongly flavored, like all sea birds' eggs, but are not unpalatable, and are esteemed by some as superior in the making of cakes and pies. When the weather is calm and warm, and the lazy, glassy ocean slowly heaves, like the breathing of some gigantic, sentient being, the Murre basks quietly in the semi-tropical sun, sleepily enjoying the renewed vitality that the sun sends through every living thing; slowly blinking and raising their feathers in the fervid rays, with a half-uttered note of lazy comfort, recuperating for the bristling activity of the coming winds and dashing, foam-crested breakers. Then the Murre is in his element. When the long-sailing, weather-beaten ships look anxiously for the brave little pilot; when every craft—even the Italian fisherman—seeks the haven, then the Murre revels in undisturbed possession, and wildly screams his exultation as he dashes into the seething foam of the thundering breakers, wresting his finny prey from where no boat could live; disappearing in the roaring waters, and remaining so long submerged that the spectator, who watches his fearless dive, has long given him up for lost, when suddenly he rises above the commotion of water, poises an instant to shake the brine from his oily overcoat, then soars away with his food and the meal for his expectant fledglings, awaiting in some nook, crevice, fissure, niche, or projecting inequality, where a nest can hold two of those callow, auk bipeds.

We gaze, and wonder if Drake and his men stood, in 1579, where we now stand, watching the whilom projectors of this busy colony; if the Farallones were here in the days of Queen Bess' favorite admiral, which we greatly doubt; as Sir Francis' log says: "We hunted along the coast (on land) from our winter quarters (Drake's Bay), and found the coast to be," etc., etc., describing it; and, as Drake's Bay is only thirty miles north of the entrance of San Francisco harbor, and he found no harbor, nor yet the Farallones, it is very reasonable to believe that the convulsion of Nature which rent those dry, perpendicular, broken cliffs, on which we look as we ride along the southern head, came subsequent to Drake's visit, or even that of La Perouse; and in that fearful hour the home of our feathered tribe rose, all dark and dripping, from the astonished Neptune's long embrace. Certainly this abrupt, little, solitary island could not have been overlooked by an exploring party passing an entire winter, only thirty miles away, where it is visible every clear day. No! on the whole, we think the birds' nests were not here in Sir Francis's time.

How curious are the many natural formations of rock: the little arches, the port-holes, bastions, niches, battlements, towers, walled sentry boxes; that natural bridge, with its sharply defined crossway and high-sprung arch. See the crowd of birds on its railed edge. They stand so close and regular that, in the distance, they seem like some grass or vegetation growing there. What a singular effect is produced, as the snow-white breakers rush, roaring up the deep chasm, spanned by this firm bit of Nature's masonry; the leaping, seething foam hides the blue ocean, clear away to the horizon, giving to our vision only the sky above the flying, fleecy froth, chafing forever at the bridge's immovable foundations—forever falling back, baffled and defeated, and still again returning, as Hope fights Fate, in useless, but in undying courage.

It is good for the intermural dweller, whose life, actions and thoughts have been year after year bounded by the Pueblo limits, to come here, and with long, grateful inhalations of old Ocean's salty breath, expand the thoracic muscles, win fresh vitality and new ammunition for the wasting tissues of his body, and, perchance, a healthful, introspective hour for the mental faculties, too often warped and distorted by long lingering "in the busy marts of men."

CONCLUSION.

Many of the buildings of '49 and '50 are still standing in their original positions. We find most of them in the northern part of the city. Some of them show little, if any change, outwardly. Their time-worn, old fashion appearance adds to their interest. Some of them are high up above the street-grade of to-day, perched upon cliffs, made by mortal hands—by political chicanery—to reward, by means of street contracts, the firm and faithful. Away up the long-reaching, repeated flights of stairs, where the old dwellings now stand, we used to walk along the natural grade. City surveys have not improved it, nor forced these faithful old homes to leave their premises. We cannot but rejoice in their tenacity—their firm adherence to the old spot, in spite of every scheme to oust and render them worthless. Sometimes we come upon one of the old, familiar dwellings, upon some street whose grade has not been changed— some old homestead, standing so unassumingly amid its pretentious, obtrusive neighbors, in their uniform of stucco-work ornamentation, and flashing plate glass, like files of nicely-decked soldiers on dress parade, and so completely changing all the old, once familiar ground, that, when we suddenly recognize our time-honored, old acquaintance, for the moment we are greatly puzzled to decide whether the mountain has come to Mohammed, or *vice versa*. Occasionally, in our peregrinations, we are startled by confronting, upon some newly-opened way in the sands beyond Market street, the well-known features of some once grand edifice, grown venerable in years of service on an old, central thoroughfare. A sense of the ludicrous close jostles our surprise, as if, led by impecuniosity to *our uncle's office*, we came upon Ralston or Hayward, furtively concealing something, and trying to seem calmly indifferent. There is something touching in the sight of an old dwelling-house in San Francisco—old for this city, where the strange vicissitudes of many years of ordinary life are rolled in one. Their time-worn fronts seem like the pleasant faces of old friends. We love to look upon their vine-clad porches, so full of interesting reminiscences — the sheltering, glazed verandas, along whose sounding floors in by-gone years pattered so many little feet—some treading now in the firm step of manhood, and others carried out, so still and white, through the old gate, long years ago, to rest forever. Those little window-panes have many times reflected the conflagration's lurid flames, and revealed the happier picture of the young wife's welcoming face, and smiles of curly-pate children. The green-gray roof, the low-ceiled rooms—each sanctified by its own history of joy or sorrow, of birth and death, and parting words and farewell kiss.

We cling to everything of good belonging to the spring of '50. If we admit that change is progress, and that progress is improvement, 'tis with a sigh that we confess it. With kindness in our hearts toward every one, we still remember those old words, "Old books to read, old wine to drink, old wood to burn, and old friends to talk with;" and we may be forgiven for clinging to the old associations and the men belonging to San Francisco in the Spring of '50.

www.ingramcontent.com/pod-product-compliance
Lightning Source LLC
Chambersburg PA
CBHW031327230426
43670CB00006B/260